THE HUMANITY TRIGGER

ON THE ORIGINS OF ANTI-SPECIESISM BY MEANS OF DIRECT ACTION
A HISTORY OF RADICAL ACTION FOR ANIMALS IN IRELAND 1822-2022

MARK HUMANITY

THE HUMANITY TRIGGER

ON THE ORIGINS OF ANTI-SPECIESISM BY MEANS OF DIRECT ACTION

A HISTORY OF RADICAL ACTION FOR ANIMALS IN IRELAND 1822-2022

© Earth Island Books

ISBN: 9781916864047 (paperback) / 9781916864054 (ebook)

Cover and interior layout by Welly Artcore
artcorefanzine@gmail.com
Original art by Mark Humanity

10 9 8 7 6 5 4 3 2 1

Published by Earth Island Books
Pickforde Lodge
Pickforde Lane
Ticehurst
TN5 7BN
www.earthislandbooks.com

Printed in the U.K.

THE HUMANITY TRIGGER

ON THE ORIGINS OF ANTI-SPECIESISM BY MEANS OF DIRECT ACTION
A HISTORY OF RADICAL ACTION FOR ANIMALS IN IRELAND 1822-2022

MARK HUMANITY

"As an Irish citizen myself, by virtue of my mother being Irish, I found this book particularly fascinating, interesting, and informative, and I was very pleasantly surprised to learn of the considerable amount of action for animal liberation that has taken place in Ireland. You don't have to be Irish to find it a great read though, and I would recommend it to anyone who desires to see other animals freed from human tyranny."

Ronnie Lee

Co-founder of the Animal Liberation Front and lifelong advocate for animals, 2023

(MAL)CONTENTS

OZYMANDIAS

I met a traveller from an antique land,

Who said—"Two vast and trunkless legs of stone

Stand in the desert. . . . Near them, on the sand,

Half sunk a shattered visage lies, whose frown,

And wrinkled lip, and sneer of cold command,

Tell that its sculptor well those passions read

Which yet survive, stamped on these lifeless things,

The hand that mocked them, and the heart that fed;

And on the pedestal, these words appear:

My name is Ozymandias, King of Kings;

Look on my Works, ye Mighty, and despair!

Nothing beside remains. Round the decay

Of that colossal Wreck, boundless and bare

The lone and level sands stretch far away."

Percy Bysshe Shelley*, 1819

*himself a vegetarian

ALL SYSTEMS GO

"What is to give light must endure burning."

Viktor Frankl, Holocaust Survivor.

FOREWORDS!

ABOUT THIS BOOK / SOURCES / DISCLAIMER

This book tells the rich story of the struggle against violence against animals in Ireland since records began but with an emphasis on the 200-year period between 1822 and 2022. It was in 1822 that the world's first Law protecting some animal species from 'unnecessary' suffering was enacted. This began a process of actions, from the State and Civil society, designed to protect non-human animals from gratuitous violence from people. What exactly constitutes unnecessary and gratuitous violence has broadened over time.

Evolving alongside the anti-Slavery and Women's Rights movements and with many overlapping adherents, the struggle for animal rights has always included the tactic of Direct Action, both non-violent and otherwise, legal and not. Ireland, and the Irish diaspora, have played pivotal roles in the development and history of the animal rights movement from its very inception in the 19th century onwards. This is the story of those individuals who braved frequent mockery and sometimes violence by taking decisive action for animals using the resources to hand. They discovered that the antidote to despair is action. Direct Action.

The idea for this book unfurled slowly as I was doing some research for a Podcast I was invited to speak on called 'Policed'.

'Policed' was a regular podcast that delved into experiences various people have had with the Police (the Gardai) in the Republic of Ireland. In early 2021 I was invited on by the Podcasts host, the late Dr. Vicky Conway (RIP), to talk about my interactions with the Police when I was a Hunt Saboteur in Galway, in the mid-1990's.

Before this interview I was researching what had become of the nascent hunt sabotage movement in Ireland since I emigrated.

Seven months before I left the country for a new life in England in late 1996, I had helped organise a 'hit' on the Galway Blazers Foxhunt. This was our third time 'sabbing'' them that season and part of a fresh wave of hunt sabotage in the Republic. Hunt sabotage has existed in Ireland since the early 1980's but took a while to spread beyond Belfast and Dublin.

That day in January 1996 we were ferociously attacked by the Hunt and their supporters in a planned ambush in front of the police. We tried to prosecute but were denied a case by the DPP due to 'lack of evidence'. Our group disbanded soon after.

Although I immediately got involved with the much larger and older Hunt Sabotage movement in the UK, I lost contact with what was going on, or not, in Ireland. All I knew for certain was that Hunt sabotage in the west of the Country was on hold following our experiences there.

My research led me quickly to a website called the Irish Newspaper Archive, an online library of almost every newspaper printed in Ireland since newspapers began. Beginning with the Belfast Telegraph in 1738, the Archive contains almost three hundred years of newspaper content.

Keywords typed into the Archives search engine like 'hunt sabotage' and 'animal liberation' yielded hundreds upon hundreds of results. From single paragraphs in parochial newspapers describing some small act of vandalism to a fur shop through to centre page features in national newspapers on the rise of animal rights militancy across the country, and everything in between. Opinion pieces, editorials, letters – some supportive, most not-, ALF press releases that read more like guerrilla communiques, interviews with anonymous activists, outrage and threats from armed farmers and butchers, condemnation by Police and Politicians, it was all there. The few newspapers not included in the Archive, such as the Galway Advertiser, have their own online archives and I scoured these for information also.

A similar online library of global radical and animal rights-oriented literature helped corroborate and expand the narrative. The Talon Conspiracy, run by vegan activist (and ex-animal rights prisoner) Josh Harper, contains thousands of publications from hundreds of different eco/anarchist/animal rights-type publications from around the world across decades of time that would otherwise have faded into historical oblivion.

These 'zines and periodicals provided another fascinating insight into the vibrancy of the animal rights history in Ireland. Before the internet, above-ground groups like the UK Animal Liberation Front Supporters Group published regular Diary of Action newsletters that listed acts of sabotage and liberation from around the world. Dogged by imprisonment for incitement, these newsletters appeared in different formats throughout the 1980's and 90's and have since been surpassed by more anonymous – and less inciteful - online resources like Bite Back and Unoffensive Animal.

Another rich seam of information was the quarterly HOWL magazine, the media wing of the mighty UK Hunt Saboteurs Association and in continuous print since 1973. All 124 (and counting) issues of HOWL are now archived on their website and many issues carried news from Ireland regarding hunt sabotage here.

With all these sources, I was able to build up a chronology of events, a timeline of every reported direct action for animals in Ireland since public records began. The definition of 'Direct Action' here is any action done by an individual or a group in which the actors use their power to directly reach certain goals of interest, in this case animal rights. Direct Action is the opposite of Indirect Action such as demonstrating or voting. Indirect Action has its place too, of course, and history shows campaigns can be most effective when both approaches are employed simultaneously. The campaign against the fur industry is a good example of this.

So, for a Politician like Richard Martin, pushing a pro-animal Bill through the legislative system until it becomes Law is a type of direct action, given his position in Society. Of course, if your Richard Martin you'll also be shooting people who abuse animals in the face, and this too is a type of direct action, though not one that was ever repeated.

Opening a vegan restaurant is also a form of direct action if that's an option available to you. If the only resource to hand is a brick, then smashing the windows of a McDonalds restaurant is direct action.

Of course, this chronology of events is incomplete as it represents only what was publicly reported. Lots of ALF-type actions probably went unmentioned in any media for two main reasons – activists might be reluctant to further expose themselves to arrest by reporting an action, or a targeted company or individual might stay silent to avoid media scrutiny and increased insurance premium costs. Therefore, what's in here is *the least* of what occurred.

Although the historical record of direct actions for animals in Ireland dates to at least the 18th Century with Richard Martin, MP, it wasn't until the formation of the Animal Liberation Front (ALF) in 1982 that a persistent campaign of economic sabotage and animal liberation swept the country over a 30-year period. It is fair to say this tactic has been in decline here and globally since around 2010.

At its peak from the mid-1980's to the late 1990's, the ALF in Ireland were typically conducting a dozen or more recorded actions every month, sustained over years. Gardai estimated there were about 100 ALF activists operating in the Republic in 1986 - an absolutely tiny figure in a population of 3.5 million at the time.

Nowadays there are perhaps one or two actions per year at most. Some years pass with zero recorded actions.

Other tactics, such as the Open Rescue method of Meat the Victims have gained traction. They have successfully and publicly trespassed several farms over the last few years, recording evidence of mistreatment and cruelty and publicising it widely. Unlike the ALF, they act in large groups and in broad daylight, using weight of numbers to access the animal housing. In their most recent action, after gathering the evidence they wanted, the activists took one pig with them as they left. The police there did not intervene. Open Rescue isn't a new tactic by any means but had gone out of fashion after a brief and dynamic period in the early 1980's in Britain with the Animal Liberation Leagues. The civil disobedience approach of Animal Rising is another current phenomenon and most closely resembles the Civil Rights tactics of the 1960's/70's.

Hunt Sabotage remains a regular occurrence in Ireland, on both sides of the border despite hunting with dogs being illegal in the UK since 2004. The only occasion Northern Irish Unionists are happy to have different laws to 'the mainland' is when it comes to killing animals it seems.

I'm happy to report even the Galway Blazers Fox Hunt continue getting hit, with a new Sab group operating against them since 2019.

I continued hunt sabbing when I emigrated to England in 1996 and until I moved again in 2003. By then, having sabbed perhaps a hundred or more hunts over an 8-year period, I was keen to move on and use that energy elsewhere. Hunting with dogs was banned by the New Labour government the following year.

I got involved with the blossoming anti-globalisation movement and writing for Brighton's best – and only - anarchist weekly, Schnews.

At this time, hunt sabotage seemed like a parochial concern when weighed against world events. All that time and energy, all that stress and aggro, the countless arrests, beatings (given and taken), even killings (two hunt sabs and one hunt thug), just to save a fox?

Fox Hunting isn't even a leading cause of fox mortality. Far more foxes are killed by cars on the road every year. A lot more foxes would be saved by us stopping road building projects than by stopping hunting. Why all this focus on an issue that isn't big, statistically, in comparison to factory farming or the climate crisis or a hundred other issues I could mention?

I rediscovered why Hunt Sabotage is important, vital even, when I researched the HOWL archive for this book. Hunt Sabotage is about redrawing a line in the sand, dividing the acceptable from the unacceptable, and placing sport hunting, as a practice, irredeemably on the wrong side of that line. The Anti-Hunt direct action movement have forced a vital shift in the paradigm. They established a psychological beachhead in the public imagination, normalising and demonstrating the idea that 'ordinary' people can and should physically intervene to protect non-human animals from people.

The movements hub, the self-financing UK-based Hunt Saboteurs Association (HSA), has retained its fiercely independent and consistent position on animal rights and the imperative of direct action, refusing to become more moderate and tokenistic like Greenpeace, despite attempts in the late 1980's. Unlike the RSPCA and League Against Cruel Sports, they never flip-flopped when it came to blood sports like fishing or falconry.

Their laser-like focus on wildlife defence has generated continued success since its inception. The ability to galvanise tens of thousands of people from all walks of life over sixty years (and counting) proves this is an idea whose time has come and that won't go away.

Almost from scratch this movement rose to take on the conceited might of the aristocracy and their mercenary supporters. Since the formation of the HSA in 1963 some of the worst excesses of human behaviour toward animals have been challenged and faced down despite often overwhelming violence.

First learning the mechanics of hunting in all it various forms, the Saboteurs then experimented with ways of scuppering the Hunt to prevent a kill. They also learned how to navigate an often heavily biased Police and media, alongside rabidly violent hunt supporters. Despite the odds, these early pioneers opened a new front in the struggle against animal abuse. Their brave persistence shifted social attitudes toward hunting and animal concerns in general. They helped make it first an issue, then an outrage, then a pariah and, since 2004 in Great Britain at least, a crime. It took half a century, but their tenacity paid off.

All that on a shoestring budget and no paid staff. They've barely ever even had a physical office. For all this and more, the Hunt Saboteurs Association deserve a standing ovation, a slap on the back and if people still wore bowler hats, we should be throwing them in the air whilst cheering.

The other main player in this history is the Animal Liberation Front which began here in earnest in 1982. They continue to operate to this day, if only sporadically, but their apex was from the mid-1980's until about 2010 when many small ALF cells operated across the country on both sides of the border.

Other groups pop up once then disappear from the historical record. The Green Moles, the Wildlife Action Group, the Hunt Retribution Squad, to name a few. The mighty Sea Shepherd make frequent appearances in the early 1980's then also disappears, off to ram and scuttle whaling ships further afield.

The difference in tactics between these groups and the likes of Greenpeace can be explained by the fundamental difference in their views on animals. Greenpeace are concerned with the survival of species (conservationism), the ALF and adjacent groups are concerned with the survival of individual sentient beings (animal rights). In practical terms, these different ideological positions are best illustrated by historical example – in the 1980's when the Norwegian Government announced plans to kill 5000 whales that year, Greenpeace and Sea Shepherd both pledged to sabotage the cull. When the Norwegians backed down a little and reduced the kill quota to 2000, Greenpeace called off their campaign as the species was no longer in danger. The Sea Shepherd, on the other hand, doubled their efforts to intercept and interfere with the whalers, concerned as they were that Greenpeace had pulled out and 2000 individual whales were still threatened.

above -*Symbol of the* **Animal Liberation Front** *and reflective of the movement's anarchist roots. This symbol could be seen adorning the backs of jackets, shop windows, butchers' vans and random walls across Britain and Ireland throughout the 1980's and 90's. stock image.*

On the issue of violence, what's surprising is the lack of it, at least from the activist community. Both the ALF and the HSA have a policy of non-violence except for self-defence and have, by and large, adhered to it. They are far more likely to be victims of violence, particularly the hunt saboteurs.

Of course, there has been lots and lots of property damage and if one considers this to be violence then so be it but let's be objective about this and bear in mind the body count is all on the oppositions side. In its 50 years of operation the ALF hasn't killed or seriously injured anyone. In that same time the meat, fish and dairy industries have a combined death count in the trillions and have helped push our planetary life-support systems to the brink of collapse. In my many years debating with perhaps hundreds of people about animals, I've learned that the sort of person who complains about the' violence' of ALF-style direct action is usually the same person who doesn't give two shits about the inherent violence to nature and animals committed every second by the animal agriculture. If the destruction of animal abusers' property is more offensive to you than the cruel destruction of sentient life, then you'll be paid well as an opinion piece writer in some of the Irish media.

Speaking of which.

Beyond the reports on ALF actions in the Irish media were the many editorials, opinion pieces and book reviews regarding the issue. These provided insight into how people outside of the activist milieu often see things. Opinions were typically confused, conformist and condemnatory yet often reached very sympathetic conclusions despite themselves. Acting assertively in defence of an animal, unless that animal happened to be your pet, genuinely perplexed most journalists. These seemed to be acts of extremity driven by madness, not by compassion. Cruelty, they'll concede, exists, particularly in the fur trade, but Shock! Horror! should anyone *do* something about it. However, some editors/journalists had the insight to recognise societies indifference to non-human animal suffering and how that might drive those concerned for animals to despair and action. Some even went well beyond the ALF in their conclusions.

Allow esteemed British author Brian Masters to illustrate my point.

Masters was reviewing two books for Dublin's Evening Press newspaper in 1989 - 'Animal Warfare-the story of the Animal Liberation Front', written by David Henshaw, a UK-based investigate journalist, and 'Sacred Elephant', about human-elephant interactions over history, by English poet and actor Heathcote Williams.

'Animal Warfare' was (badly) researched and written in 1989, when attacks by the ALF and similar groups were becoming more audacious and destructive. For a right-wing hack like Henshaw there was plenty to get outraged about. The Hunt Retribution Squad had recently vandalised the grave of the Duke of Beaufort, an avid foxhunter in his day. Fires on a scale not seen since the Blitz engulfed department stores selling fur coats. Hundreds stormed vivisection laboratories to take away animals and information. Food-poisoning hoaxes, like the Mars Bar scare, shocked and angered the public and cost Manufacturers millions. Henshaw describes it all with contempt. Some actions did indeed go too far, and only served to alienate further an already bemused populace, but property damage aside most actions were non-violent and proportionate. Henshaw, however, cannot step outside of his own ideological framework even briefly, for a more objective look round, and remains appalled by everything said and done by 'the extremists'. It's all 'sinister', even down to the round-rimmed spectacles of one of the activists.

Masters describes it well in his review but fails to recognise his own inconsistencies. The review is worth quoting in full:

"Few now quarrel with the proposition that humankind, an upstart species in evolutionary terms, exercises absolute tyranny over the rest of creation. Most regard this as the natural order of things, ordained by one deity or another, and remain unperturbed by the vision of a moribund planet upon which humans will enjoy their conquest in loneliness of spirit.

Others view it withs a shuddering sense of belated moral responsibility and try valiantly to alter direction – these are the mixed bag of philosophers, fascists, and little old ladies, who form the troops of the various animal welfare and liberation armies of recent years.

In Animal Warfare, David Henshaw has traced their origins and purposes thoroughly.

All of them are here, from hunt saboteurs to letter-bombers, their earnest and passionate progress chronicled if not honoured. Henshaw legitimately questions how many anti-vivisectionists refuse a vaccination jab on principle. But for the first time, scientists who cut up living creatures have been forced to justify themselves on both utilitarian and ethical grounds. That is something.

However, Henshaw is the wrong man for the task. He is entirely without sympathy for the people he writes about. Of course, the extremists in their balaclavas are ridiculous, and their terrorist tactics sinister.

It is also true that many of them are motivated by a coruscating, unproductive hatred. But the philosophy of most animal defenders deserves a respect which Henshaw is unwilling or unable to allow.

The trouble is that Henshaw subscribes to the widespread prejudice that human life is sacred, or at least special. And it follows from such a premise that the murder of one individual is evil, while the systematic murder of thousands of other creatures is merely regrettable.

Anthropocentric arrogance leads to the sort of tragedy revealed in Sacred Elephant, a powerful and pathetic book only slightly spoiled by Heathcote William's pseudo-poetic ramblings. The second half is an anthology of fact and opinion about the elephant, 60 million years in the making and soon to be extinguished by human greed, and hubris.

The elephant is intelligent, socially sophisticated, and sensitive. In distress it weeps tears. It knows remorse. And it takes a very long time to kill.

There are some terrible pictures in this book. The worst shows a hunter amidst a herd which he is slowly slaughtering for fun. If I were to witness an event like that, I have little doubt that I would wrest the man's gun from him and blast his soulless carcass into wretched oblivion. Does that make me the terrorist, or him?

Pick a lane, Brian. Are people who stand up for animals hate-filled fascists and little old ladies or are we not going far enough, and we should be blasting hunters to oblivion with shotguns? You can't have it both ways mate.

Henshaw was indeed the 'wrong man 'for the task of investigating the Animal Liberation Front and adjacent groups. Every page drips with his dismissive, cynical attitude and he remains utterly unmoved by the concerns of the activists or the plight of the animals. Henshaw offers a description of a movement plagued by 'fascists and little old ladies' and obsessed with predictions of a doomed humanity unless we all convert to veganism. He implies such predictions were indicative of an extremist mindset, proof of how deluded the vegans are. Here he couldn't be more wrong. Fast forward 30 years or so and the science is in - turns out animal agriculture *is* killing us and the planet and must be replaced by non-disastrous methods of farming if we stand a chance of retaining a viable biosphere. Meat isn't just murder, it also suicide, genocide, and ecocide.

As for fascists.... the far-right did try to infiltrate the animal rights scene at this time, with groups like the National Front pushing an animal welfare agenda and encouraging its memebers to join local animal rights groups, attend demos and try and introduce racist ideas to the movement. Occasionally a skinhead in a Union Jack t-shirt would turn up at a demo outside a circus or a slaughterhouse, chanting along with everyone else. The much larger anarchist contingent also typically present at such events soon led the charge in expelling these individuals and the tactic quickly faded. There was one notable fascist presence however (no, not Hitler).

David McCalden, a Northern Irish National Front organiser, and Holocaust denier and also on the committee of the Hunt Saboteurs Association. In fact, he edited the very first edition of HOWL, the Hunt Sabs magazine, back in 1973. Contained in its slim four pages is a full-page article on how Halal and Kosher animal slaughter is cruel (Christian slaughter is fine), a paragraph praising a new National Front policy opposing bloodsports, and a letter from Herr Dave himself explaining (atrociously) why humans are biologically designed to eat meat. His 'arguments', such as they are, are a hilarious thought-salad of the sort of things you might hear from a drunk Uncle at a wedding, like "If humans stopped eating meat the world over, disaster would ensue" and "Human beings are in the schizoid predicament of being half-human and half-animal. It would be folly to pretend otherwise." Risking folly, might I suggest that human beings are both fully human *and* fully animal?

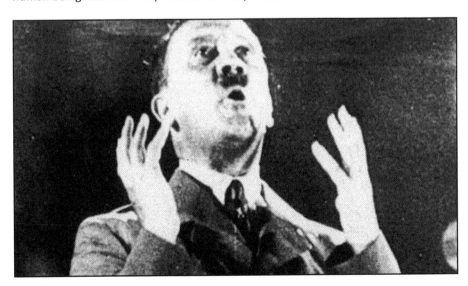

above – *artists impression of David McCalden, * 1951-1990, AKA "Revisionist Dave", one time editor of both HOWL and the National Fronts Nationalist News. Stock image.*

McCalden continued as HOWL's editor for another two years, but no trace of his bigoted personality is obvious beyond issue One. He was kicked out of the movement in 1978 and left for the USA where he helped set up a book publishing company that specialised in holocaust denial literature. He even put up a $50,000 'reward' for anyone who could prove that Jews were gassed at Auschwitz. When Auschwitz survivor Mel Mermelstein took him up on the offer, McCalden refused to engage with him.

Most Saboteurs across the UK were enraged by McCaldens views. While many were meat eaters themselves, McCaldens obvious racism was too much to bear.

A few were of the opinion that the animals do not care about the race politics of the person who saves them, and the movement, small as it was then, couldn't afford to shed members because of this. Should we also expel members who ate meat? Or drink milk? Or vote Tory?

This kickstarted a well-overdue debate that culminated in McCalden being voted off the HSA committee and out of the movement generally in 1979.

McCalden then emigrated to the USA, co-establishing the Institute for Historical Review, a book publishing company that specialised in Holocaust denial literature, before dying of AIDS in 1990, aged 39. A most unlikely disease to befall a member of the master race.

Such poor-sighted ambiguity about working with members of the far-right was a gift to a hostile media and a total turn-off to all but for other racists. Animals might not know or care about the race politics of the human helping them, but People care about this and rightly so, and the movement requires People.

However, the movement addressed and rectified their mistake and any notions about working with the far right are long gone.

Following McCaldens ousting, the HSA publicly affiliated with Anti-Fascist Action (the precursor to today's Antifa/Anteefa) and declared the direct-action movement for animals a 'no-go' area for fascists. Nowadays you are as likely to find hunt saboteurs physically engaging with the far right as you are with a hunt.

above - *Anti-Fascist (center) fighting his way through a mob of Nazi Skins at the Battle of Waterloo, London, September 1992.source AFA archive.*

above - ***THEY GOT THE GUNS BUT WE GOT THE NUMBERS.*** *Huntsman stampedes his horse into a group of Hunt Saboteurs, Nottingham, circa 1996, used with permission from A. Testa.*

Politically, the animal rights movement in Ireland generally had few to no supporters in the corridors of power over the century of the Republic's existence. Sure, we had a successful revolution against one of the biggest Empires the world has ever known in 1922 but "we were the most conservative revolutionaries in history", as the then Minister for Justice Kevin O'Higgins said. There have often been individual politicians like the late independent TD Tony Gregory who have tried to force Bills through the Dail to have things like Coursing banned but they remain a tiny minority. This is a nation that has, until very recently, been as politically frozen as the old Soviet Union used to be. A duopoly of power shared between two Political Parties so identical that they more closely resemble two wings of the same Party- and both ultimately controlled by a lecherous Catholic Church. This unholy trinity dominated Irish society for a century. Anti-intellectual and deeply authoritarian, corrupt and dogmatic, highly defensive, brittle and aggressive, the Church came complete with a Cult of personality in the face of the Pope and his emissaries of Bishops and an army of Priests.

Ireland has changed so much in the last 30 years or so that its worth remembering just how conservative and stifling life was for most of the 20th century.

Socially – until recently – Ireland was rabidly and often hysterically anti -homosexual, anti-Semitic, anti-communist, anti-feminist, and anti-individualist. Women were treated as second-class citizens, children third-class. Almost uniformly Catholic, white, and patriarchal, we even had our own concentration camp system to rival the Gulag. The Magdalene Laundries and the Mother and Baby Homes network, both run by the nuns, enslaved tens of thousands of Irish girls and young women who had transgressed the countries sanctimonious attitudes to sex and marriage. Described by the Courts as 'first-time offenders' and imprisoned for years, they watched powerless as their babies were sold to rich Americans. Child abuse and rape was rife but deliberately ignored throughout the nation's homes and institutions. Catholicism has many political shades including left-wing, even explicitly anarchist strains (see Dorothy Day and the Catholic Worker movement), but the correlation between the formal Catholic Church and fascism are impossible to overlook and hard to overstate.

Divorce, abortion, even contraception were all illegal until recently. Until 1992, even *discussing* these issues on any public forum was illegal. Being gay was a crime until 1993.

"We were the most conservative Revolutionaries in history" K. O'Higgins on the
Fight against British Imperialism, led by this man above - **Eamonn de Valera** *('Dev')*,
1882-1975, anti-Imperialist Nationalist Irish Catholic, seen here in traditional **Native
American Chippawa** *Chief head dress in 1919. This complex man, one of Irelands
most famous sons, is rumoured by some to be the bastard love child of* **John Gubbins**
and Dev's mum, **Catherine Coll** *(they certainly have similar nose and chin). Ms Coll
came from Bruree and worked as a maid for Gubbins prior to her departure for New
York, where Dev was born. stock image.*

DeValera was made an honorary Chief of the Chippawa Tribe because of his vocal support of Native American rights. "Though I am white, I am not of the English race" he told a cheering crowd at the Tribal ceremony. De Valera pops up again later in this story.

Censorship, enforced by various State bodies and the Church, tightly regulated what the population read and watched.

Movies like "Monkey Business' by the Marx Brothers was banned when it came out in 1931 in case it encouraged 'anarchic tendencies.' Witnessing Monty Pythons 'the Life of Brian' on smuggled-in video cassettes guaranteed you a one-way ticket to hell. 'Playboy' was a crime until 1995, as were books like 'Brave New World and 'The Catcher in the Rye'. If it criticized the Church or showed too much ankle, it was strictly *verboten*. When I was growing up, the closest materiel one could procure to assist in nocturnal emissions were the odd photograph of ladies in bikinis from those free holiday travel brochures your Dad used to bring home in Spring, apparently.

The **Committee on Evil Literature**, established in 1926, saw these bans strictly enforced. The Arts had to live up to the 'holiest traditions', as De Valera put it. There was even a successful campaign, led by the Church, to ban jazz from radio and dancehalls in the 1930's, leading to a virtual ban on jazz music at dances for years. The GAA forbade their members from even watching 'foreign' sports like soccer, cricket, hockey and rugby, never mind playing them. Spies would attend such games and spot for any GAA members secretly enjoying the spectacle. These members would be fined by their local GAA club if caught. This rule, Rule #27, was lifted in 1971.

From the very get-go, a 'marketplace of ideas' the Republic of Ireland was not, neither politically nor culturally.

Economically, the Republic began, as Fintin O'Toole put it, as "a vast cattle ranch with a few cities and a lot of small provincial towns attached". From the Free States inception in 1922 until the Corporatization of the economy in the 1960's, the new Nation remained largely impoverished and socially static.

From the 1960's on, Irelands economy became beholden to global Corporations who settled here for its absurdly low corporate tax rate and mostly non-Unionized, largely apolitical but educated workforce. A Faustian Pact of economic incentives are all geared toward providing an attractive base for global capital. Again, until recently with the rise of Sinn Fein, Ireland barely had a cohesive or effective left-wing. The Irish State even successfully took the EU to Court to *avoid* receiving $13 BILLION in taxes owed to them by Apple in 2016. Tax, after all, is something only the *little people* pay.

So, for most of the Free States existence, Ireland had at least as much in common with a type of non-expansionist/parochial fascism (an idea originally called Corporatism by

Mussolini and similar to Franco's Spain or Salazar's dictatorship in Portugal) as it did with its formal position as an open, Democratic Republic.

Indeed, a major figure in the early formation of the Republic, Eoin O'Duffy, was an explicit fascist and prior to his fall from grace in the 1930's towered over many of the new Nations institutions – O'Duffy was first leader of the IRA in Ulster, then head of the new Police force, then Chief of Staff of the National Army. He was also, at various points, a TD for Sinn Fein and Fine Gael, a Party he helped establish and initially lead. He was also highly influential in the GAA and was on the Irish Olympic Committee. A pro-Treatyite, O'Duffy established the Army Comrades Association (ACA), a kind of precursor to the Proud Boys. The ACA engaged in punch-ups with the (now illegal and largely left-wing) IRA, who frequently broke up meetings of the ruling pro-Treaty Cumann na nGaedheal Party public meetings.

above – *the original Brew Crew – always drunk and fighting their own side - pro-fascist **Irish Brigade volunteers** in Spain 1936. "The military efficiency of this unit is **absolutely nil**" said Colonel Juan Yague, commander of Francos forces on the Madrid Front. Unless they're shooting other fascists, of course. The Brigade gained a reputation for heavy drinking and light soldiering. Stock image.*

O'Duffy had a thing for a man in uniform and was a huge admirer of Mussolini and Hitler, so much so that he formed the Irish Brigade, a 700-strong combat unit (out of 7000 volunteers), to go to Spain and help Franco fight the democratically elected leftist Republican government. This was more than any other nation. The unit soon earned a reputation for being awful at fighting but really great at getting drunk. They saw combat twice before being ordered back to Ireland in silent disgrace. Their first engagement was in a town called Ciempozuelos, just outside Madrid. As the Brigade marched into the small town they came under fire and so began a skirmish that lasted an hour until both sides realised they were on the same side. "We were attacked by a Brigade from the Canary Islands who mistook us for Reds" explained one Irishman,

Matt Becket. Four Irish Brigadiers and 13 Spanish Fascists lay dead as a result of this 'friendly fire'. At their next encounter, this time against the actual enemy, the Irish Brigade advanced on a village called Titulcia. A shell exploded amongst them as they advanced, killing six. The Brigade ran back to their trenches and flat-out refused orders to resume the attack. They were soon shipped back to Ireland. Thankfully, their only victims were other fascists and themselves. In 1943 O'Duffy wrote to Hitler offering to raise a battalion of Irish volunteers to assist the Nazis on the Eastern Front. Perhaps unwilling to risk losing valuable German troops to 'friendly fire' from O'Duffy's men, Hitler turned him down. Yet O'Duffy and his clown army weren't the only expressions of Irish fascist tendencies.

above – *ex- Garda Commissioner **Eoin O'Duffy** addresses his legion of Blueshirts, Dublin 1934. He claimed a force of 30,000 Blueshirts, with 7000 prepared to join him in Spain but only took 700 with him to fight for Franco in 1936. 700 more were prevented from joining them by De Valera's Government. The Blueshirts merged with two other right-wing parties to form Fine Gael in 1933. Stock image*

When Hitler finally did something right and blew his own brains out in a windowless bunker on April 30th, 1945, Irelands Taoiseach (Prime Minister) Eamonn De Valera publicly offered his condolences to Germany 'for their loss'. He wanted to send a letter through to Berlin but by 1945 the German post office system was less than reliable (and mostly dead) so he and Secretary of External Affairs, Joseph Walshe, went in person to the German Embassy in Dublin instead. Irelands President, Douglas Hyde, popped by the following day to repeat the offer. Details of the depths of Nazi depravity was public knowledge at this point, Auschwitz being liberated months earlier, Dachau only the week before. Only the heads of State of fellow fanatical (and Fascist) Catholics Spain and Portugal, and ultra-authoritarian (and even worse than the Nazis) Japan, expressed similar sentiment- everyone else was dancing in the street.

above left – *thousands of Irish Christian Front (ICF) supporters pre-empting Queens Radio Ga-Ga, Cork city, circa 1936/37. The crossed arms 'X' salute expressed the crowd's solidarity with fascist Franco and his army of murdering rapists. The ICF raised substantial supplies and money for Franco's army. Catholicism and fascism have long made easy bedfellows. "If it is necessary to be a fascist to defend Christianity then I am a fascist and so are my colleagues" said the Fronts leader, Fianna Fail TD Patrick Belton, (Irish Independent, 12 October 1936). Belton wanted O'Duffy's Brigade to stay in Ireland and deal with the "Reds" here instead of in Spain. Given the Brigades record of firing on their own side, this was, objectively, a good idea. Stock images.*

above right – *ex-Garda Commissioner and Hitler fanboy **Eoin O'Duffy**. O'Duffy tried and failed to orchestrate a right-wing coup in 1933 – he didn't seem to realise Ireland was already dominated by an Authoritarian dictatorship and there's only room for one at the top. Despite it all, O'Duffy received a full State funeral when he drank himself to death in 1944.*

It should be stressed that Dev's ambivalence toward fascism and adherence to diplomatic protocol was more to do with sticking it to Churchill – a man De Valera absolutely loathed - than anything else, yet dangerously naïve, nonetheless.

"He was feted by the Dublin social glitterati, including a young politician, Charles Haughey, who was later to become Ireland's most controversial prime minister." Journalist Kim Bielenberg on Nazi Otto Skorzeny's reception in Ireland, 1957.

We even provided a safe, undisturbed home for almost 200 top Nazis like Otto 'Scarface' Skorzeny (AKA 'Hitlers Favorite Soldier') and Albert Folens after WW2. It's not as if they just melted into the background either, as war criminals tend to do. They didn't even change their names. A news article in the Nationalist and Leinster Times from July 1960 even glowingly refers to Skorzeny by his former Nazi military position - "German wartime paratroop leader Colonel Otto Skorzeny" winning first prize for having the "best pair of fat lambs" at that years Athy Country Fayre. Injecting hundreds of unrepentant Nazis into the body politic of Ireland can only have shifted the tone of our culture even more Rightwards over the post-war years.

"The greatest judicial scandal of the twentieth century" Albert Folens on the Nuremburg Trials of former Nazi's, interview with Irish journalist Senan Moloney, 1987

"If you knew the number of rosaries I have said for the victory of Franco....Hitler was an angel compared to Stalin!" A. Folens, same interview

Albert Folens, top Belgian SS collaborator and war criminal, established the still-running Folens' educational book publishers after escaping from a Belgian prison where he was serving 10 years for collaboration with the Nazi regime. Fritz Golee, a Belgian Judge dealing with collaborators after the War, described Folens as a" very active propagandist for Nazi policies". His publishing company has been providing the Irish school system with most of its standard curriculum books since 1958, including History books. Bet you were never taught that in school! His books are *still* being read by Irish kids! He must be the most widely read Nazi since Hitler! Prior to providing books to every school in the Republic, he was a teacher in Dublin and another future Taoiseach – Alan Dukes – was one of his students.

The Irish State worked to set these monsters free!

"He regularly attended Madrid memorial services to pray for the souls of Hitler and Mussolini" Obituary to Otto Skorzeny, Irish Independent, July 8th, 1975.

The same thousand million welcomes were firmly *not* extended to the many victims of the Nazis.

And like almost every other country on Earth, most people in Ireland held deeply speciesist attitudes toward all other non-human life. Speciesism is a 'root metaphor' – an outlook deeply marinated into the Human Psyche- and predates Fascism by millennia but both are born from the same maxim that 'might makes right'. Hitler and his followers simply extended the reach of this notion to include humans as well. The Master Species became the Master Race. And what most closely resembles the Death Camps of the Third Rich than today's abattoir?

"In relation to animals, all people are Nazis; for the animals, it is an eternal Treblinka" from The Letter Writer, 1968, Isaac Singer.

Despite such an arch-conservative, even reactionary, socio-political environment, individuals concerned for the plight of animals in Ireland began to slowly emerge and organize again in the post-war world. In a land oppressive to so many of its human inhabitants, animal oppression might easily have gone overlooked, a distant ship on the horizon. However, after an ebb in activities following World War 2, the movements second wave began in the early 1970's with the advent of Vegetarian cafes, shops, and restaurants in Ireland's bigger cities. Some were short lived; others became legendary and are still around today. A revitalized Vegetarian Society was also reestablished in Dublin in 1977 by UK-born Christopher Fettes, who also founded the Irish Green Party in 1981.

"Vegetarians come in three kinds- the ones who eat dead fish but not mammals, the real extremos who eat no animal products whatever, and the ones who eat products of the earth and dairy products." Journalist Lucille Redmond does her best at differentiating between pescatarians, vegans and vegetarians before these terms were generally known or understood. Irish Times, April 15, 1978.

Thankfully, Ireland has developed enormously since the Church began collapsing when the first whisperings of mass child abuse began to surface in the 1990's. This was followed a decade later with what was essentially the collapse of the capitalist economy in 2008 – only to be bailed out at societies expense via *'austerity measures'*, but the illusion of the 'free' market being the only game in town is no longer the Consensus.

A long-overdue paradigm shift has occurred, flipping Ireland's status from one of Europe's most conservative societies to one of its most socially progressive, all in the space a few generations. Sinn Fein are poised to take power on both sides of the border in 2025, the Catholic Church is fading quickly into oblivion and Leo Varadkar, the openly gay, secular son of a Hindu from Mumbai is Taoiseach (twice over), all unthinkable positions even just twenty years ago. Varadkar even spoke openly about reducing his consumption of red meat because of climate change and cancer issues but quickly backtracked when the Farmers got all upset.

Ireland today is a vastly different country than it used to be but most of the history included here occurred before all that. Perhaps many of the actions and events listed in this book are, in part, harbingers and symptoms of that change.

The animal advocacy movement in Ireland could now be said to be in its Fifth Wave, characterized by social media influencers, normalization of and increasing provision for 'plant-based diets' and a Civil Disobedience approach to direct action. The previous, overlapping, four Waves are detailed in Chapters 1, 2 and 3 respectively.

This story must include, in part, the history of the animal rights movement in Great Britain, as it's from there that the ALF and Hunt Saboteurs first emerged. It was British activists who helped train Irish Hunt Sabs, initially at least, and there has always been cross-pollination between the two islands, locked together by geography. Irish born activists are ubiquitous in the UK movement, and this has been the case since the movement's inception back in the 19th century. Similarly, ideas and tactics born in England, the birthplace of the modern animal rights movement, have been a constant source of inspiration and emulation to Irish activists.

This book also includes my own history within the animal rights movement and anarcho punk scene. I lived, and sabbed, in the UK for 16 years so the narrative might meander a bit between the two islands but hopefully will remain relevant and coherent.

Just a quick note specifically on fox hunting - this Pleasure Killing has nothing to do with 'controlling numbers of foxes' and is not a natural pursuit for the hounds. Nor has it anything to do with 'sport' – in a real sport, both sides know they're playing. Nor has it anything to do with helping farmers. Many, perhaps most, farmers hate them. Would you like a riot of dozens of mounted horses and hounds, plus many more hunt support following in a convoy of vehicles, plus maybe a bunch of sabs, charging through your land and scaring the bejasus out of 'your livestock', potentially spreading disease like TB as they do so?

The Hunt gets away with it because they are Establishment through and through - many top Police, Judges, Lawyers and politicians are members of Foxhunt Kennels, it's a way to connect to other members of the Elite and showcase their Dominion over everyone and everything else. Intimidation, explicit or otherwise, is frequently used to quell local opposition.

 As for 'controlling numbers' of foxes to help farmers? Utter bullshit of course - do you really think these people devote their time and money into actually helping others with their 'pest control'? Every Saturday? At their own expense? These creeps wouldn't give you the steam off their piss. No, they're a hobby and a business, not a 'pest control' charity. When farmers want to kill foxes, they employ one or two professional marksmen to do it nocturnally. Farmers do not want a bunch of half-pissed, arrogant, rich wankers taking advantage of the situation to have a joy ride and a pleasure kill on their land.

In fact, there is ample evidence of fox hunters seeking to increase the population of foxes in an area, so they have more to hunt! When required Hunts will breed foxes, to be released on the day of the hunt itself, so-called 'bagged' hunting. They even *introduced* foxes to the Isle of Wright and the slightly bigger island of Australia, just to hunt them.

They can't take enough photos of themselves posing with their 'trophy' after the kill, smiling from ear to ear, smearing the blood of the victim onto the faces of their children, cutting bits off the mangled carcass for posterity.

Because these people often own or influence large sections of the Media, they try to spin the narrative to present what they do as crucial for a healthy countryside and demanded by farmers to help stem the population of the fox. The fact of the matter is they are violent, feral vandals who seek personal gratification as the expense of others, no better than bear-baiters, just slightly better dressed.

As for hunting in general? When you find yourself on a dying planet whose wildlife population is in freefall and heading to extinction, your first thought should not be "I know, I'll kill more wildlife! for shits and giggles!".

"Probably the most revolutionary movement the world has ever known – absolutist, impossibilist, bizarre."
Guardian columnist Polly Toynbee's thoughts on the Animal Liberation Front. Not sure if its praise or condemnation.

This book began life as a website. Check out www.thehumanitytrigger.com, for lots more images and extended meanderings. This website gets updated on a regular basis.

CHAPTER ONE - IN THE BEGINNING - PRE-1822, THE FIRST WAVE (1822-1911) WORLDS FIRST ANIMAL PROTECTION LAWS, FIRST HUNT SABOTAGE.

Ireland and the Irish have many *firsts* in the history of our relations with other animals.

It was on this Island that the first two pieces of State Legislation protecting (some) animals from (some) violence from humans were Enacted.

It was an Irishman, Galway native Richard Martin, who formed the world's first Police force to enforce these laws, the RSPCA.

It was an Irish Priest, Fr. Eugene Sheehy, who organised the world's first recorded hunt sabotage, in County Limerick.

In fact, Ireland and the Irish have a deep and diverse history of acting in defence of animals and this book aims to explore that history, particularly the 200 years between 1822 and 2022, for it was in 1822 that the ground-breaking Cruelty to Cattle Act was passed, pushed through a reluctant and cynical Parliament by MP for Galway, Richard "Humanity/hair-trigger" Martin.

This Act is widely but wrongly believed to be the world's first State legislation protecting domesticated animals from "'unnecessary cruelty" from us Humans. While it's true to say that it was the first *successful* piece of legislation protecting animals, it was not the first.

That credit goes to a well-dressed chap from London named Thomas Wentworth, AKA Lord Deputy of Ireland.

above - **Thomas Wentworth,** *Lord Deputy of Ireland 1632-1639. Close but no cigar. Stock image.*

Almost 2oo years before Richard Martins 1822 Cruelty to Cattle Act was the **Wentworth Act of 1635** which criminalized "tying ploughs to horses' tails and pulling wool from live sheep". A fine of ten shillings applied. As newly appointed Lord Deputy of Ireland, Wentworth noticed these "barbaric customs", long since abandoned in his native England, were common amongst the local Gaelic farmers he now ruled over. The farmers engaged in these ancient practice's because they were incredibly poor and could not afford harnesses or shears. Upon consultation with the Irish Parliament, these acts were banned by Wentworth.

This Act became the world's first piece of State legislation outlawing violence against animals. It has since been criticised for being ineffective and just another way of taxing the Irish. It's true to say the enforcement of this law was haphazard and inefficient – the license to enforce the Act and thus collect the fines was simply sold annually for $100 to private individuals. Corruption was endemic and the cruelty persisted.

Wentworth's own justification for the Act was to prevent "cruelty used to the beasts" and for this he should be commended. However, had he, and the vampiric Empire he represented, been themselves less cruel to the native Gaels, had they allowed the Irish to prosper unhindered by nefarious demands from the Crown, these archaic farming techniques would have been long done away with, as had happened elsewhere in Europe.

Another pre-1822 individual of note is **Robert 'Linen' Cook**, 1646-1726, the only vegan in any Irish Village during his lifetime.

A wealthy and eccentric farmer from Cappaquinn, Co. Wexford, Cook made a fortune selling wool before his conversion to veganism but by the early 1690's he rejected all products of animal origin. "For many years before he died, neither ate fish, flesh, milk, butter, nor drank any kind of fermented liquor, nor wore woollen clothes, or any other produce of an animal, but linen." wrote historian Charles Smith in 1774, hence the nickname "Linen Cook". The guy practically invented Straight Edge, some 300 years before the release of Minor Threats seminal "Out of Step" LP. Ian MacKaye eat your heart out.

Influenced by Greek philosopher Pythagoras- himself a vegetarian- and the Bible, Cooks farm only had white-skinned animals and presumably these animals were fed and cared for but not exploited. On one occasion, a fox was caught by his servants as it wandered about the farm. Cook lectured the fox on the Fifth Commandment (Thou shalt not kill) and made him 'run the gauntlet' – the fox had to run through two rows of farm hands as they beat and kicked the poor thing. Cook then sent the confused and bruised creature on his way.

Another highly notable incident prior to 1822 was an infamous duel between an animal abusing scoundrel by the name of **G.R. 'Fighting' Fitzgerald** and one of the heroes of this story, the esteemed Richard Martin, MP for his native Galway, close friend of George IV, who nicknamed him Humanity Dick for his services to animals, and all round *flaneur*. Martin's other nickname was 'Hair-trigger' Martin for his predisposition to pistol duelling. He fought about 100 duels in his colourful life and had a reputation for being quick on the draw.

Martins first recorded direct action for animals was in *circa* 1781 when he challenged "Fighting" Fitzgerald to a duel. A well-known gentleman thug, Fitzgerald was infamous for his belligerence and ill-temper, thought by some to have been caused by a blow to his head when a youth.

Fitzgerald had recently fallen out with a mutual friend, the Marquess of Sligo Lord Altamont, and called round to his estate demanding "satisfaction", i.e., a duel. When Fitzgerald knocked on Altamont's door, his pet Alsatian dog was first to arrive and was immediately shot dead by Fitzgerald, who then fled.

above - **Lord Altamont's** dog shot dead by 'Fighting' Fitzgerald circa 1777. Stock image.

Martin was incensed by this act of casual cruelty but couldn't himself challenge Fitzgerald to a duel. The "'Gentleman's Code'" stated Altamont, as the aggrieved party, should do this, but he was too old and afraid.

So Martin had to wait. He waited three full years, until his chance arrived when Fitzgerald was due in Court for killing Altamont's beloved Alsatian. This was years before any laws prohibiting cruelty to animals, so Fitzgerald was being charged with damaging 'property'. Martin volunteered to represent Lord Altamont and his deceased dog *pro bono*.

Martin so publicly eviscerated Fitzgerald in Court that day, so verbally abused and belittled him for hours in the dock, that Fitzgerald had no option but to challenge Martin to a duel, which was eagerly anticipated and immediately accepted.

above - *Artist's impression of the infamous duel between* **Richard 'Trigger' Martin** *and* **G.R. 'Fighting' Fitzgerald**, *circa 1781. Round One - Martin shoots Fitzgerald in the face. Stock image.*

On the fateful day of the Duel, to be held in in Castlebar barracks, Martin and Fitzgerald, each accompanied by their manservants, took positions, and prepared to engage in potentially mortal combat. Going back-to-back, then walking set paces before turning and firing their pistols at each other, Martin's bullet struck Fitzgerald on the cheek, knocking him off his feet and sending his shot skywards.

Despite the injury, Fitzgerald immediately demanded another duel. Martin agreed, upset at not having killed his nemesis. This time, in a decidedly ungentlemanly move, 'Fighting' Fitzgerald ducked down as he turned and fired- a favoured tactic of his. He hit Martin on the shoulder. Both men then collapsed in pain and had to be dragged off the field of combat by their respective servants. This was violent, privileged animal advocacy at its best-dressed and most flamboyant. Fighting Fitzgerald was later hanged for murdering his father's attorney in 1786.

1822 - The world's second State Act protecting animals, the pivotal **Cruelty to Cattle Act** was signed into law by King George IV on the 22nd of July 1822, a time when even owning humans as slaves was perfectly legal (in Britain's colonies) and seen by many as totally normal. This is when things really get going.

Formulated and argued through Parliament by Richard 'Humanity Dick' Martin, MP for Galway, West Ireland, this Act forbade anyone to "wantonly and cruelly beat or ill-treat [any] horse, mare, gelding, mule, ass, ox, cow, heifer, steer, sheep or other cattle". Oddly, Bulls were excluded. The Act even had its very own private enforcement agency, the RSPCA, co-established by Martin in 1824. Full-time RSPCA Inspectors, complete with uniforms and batons, and paid for by Martin, would patrol London's streets and markets, looking to arrest anyone flouting the new law. Martin also acted as the RSPCA's Solicitor, prosecuting cases *pro bono* on behalf of the Society. It's worth noting the animals had a police force years before humans did. In fact, the London Metropolitan Police, established five years later in 1829, modelled their uniforms and rank structure on the RSPCAs Inspectors.

above - *Richard 'Hair-trigger" Martin, AKA 'Humanity Dick', 1754-1834.Member of Parliament for his native Galway constituency. Stock image.*

In its first year of existence, the RSPCA brought 63 people to Court for breaking the new law, all of which failed, mainly because Magistrates and Judges refused to take the charges seriously. In fact, it wasn't until 1838, after 14 years of trying, that the dam finally burst, and the RSPCA had their first successful prosecution. A trader in London named Bill Burns was fined by the Courts for beating a donkey on the street. Martin, prosecuting the case on behalf of the RSPCA and the donkey, felt compelled to bring the bruised animal into the Courthouse for all to bear witness to the wounds, so the smirking Magistrates gathered might finally sympathise with the aggrieved defendant, a scene immortalised in a painting by P.Mathews. Burns was found 'Guilty!'.

Then, snatching defeat from the jaws of victory, Martin requested the Magistrates only fine Burns the minimum amount, and Martin then paid the fine himself! Apparently, he only wished to set an example under Law, to set a precedent, not to punish anyone specifically. You'd think that after 14 years of trying, he'd be eager to stick the boot in.

Thankfully this was a one-off and the RSPCA never again paid the fines of convicted animal abusers.

The 1822 Act set the legal ball slowly rolling and it was enhanced with the passing of the **1835 Cruelty to Cattle Act**, also pushed through by the RSPCA, which extended the scope of the original Act to include badger baiting and other cruel practices. Both Acts were then superseded by Robert Peels **1849 Cruelty to Animals Act** which added the option of imprisonment to those convicted of breaking the new Act.

above - *The trial of* **Bill Burns** *– behind the donkey, thumbing his nose at Richard* **"Humanity" Martin, MP,** *on right of donkey. The Magistrates couldn't take the charges seriously until Martin brought the donkey into the Courtroom so all could bear witness to the physical trauma the animal had suffered at the hands of his "owner". After 16 years of trying, this was the first successful prosecution for animal abuse ever. Painting by P. Mathews, August 1838. Stock image.*

The **1911 Protection of Animals Act** expanded further the range of protected animals and slightly increased the severity of punishments available to Magistrates. The Irish Free State, formed in 1922, retained this Act, with minor amendments added on over time, until the **2014 Animal Health and Welfare Act**. While a small step in the right direction, the cloudy wording and large loopholes in the Act mean intensive animal agriculture can continue unabated. If you kick your pet chicken because your bored, you're a criminal. If you imprison ten thousand chickens in a windowless room then sell their tortured bodies, you're an entrepreneur.

It must be noted here that the 1849 Act was not the first time animal abusers could end up in prison for their misdeeds — a ruined Viking-era tower on a tiny islet in the middle of Ballynahinch Lough in the remote West of Ireland served as an unofficial prison for local animal abusers.

Owned and operated by the region's Landlord, Richard Martin (who else), Martin had secured the 'right' to draft and enforce his own laws on his private Estate and acted as Judge, Jury, and Jailer to those whom he convicted. He personally rowed the offenders out to the old tower himself, hectoring the prisoner for their transgressions all the way. Legend has it he was particularly harsh on those who mistreated donkeys.

"Trigger" Martin, MP, was centuries ahead of his time when it came to animal abuse. Prior to the Act of 1822, Martin was known to row local animal abusers out to this tower on a tiny islet in the middle of Ballynahinch Lough in West Galway until they repented for their misdeeds (above). He was particularly harsh on anyone who mistreated donkeys it seems. Stock image.

And in his spare time, Humanity Dick liked nothing more than to hunt down and kill foxes. For fun. You know, he needed to work off the stress of prosecuting donkey-beaters with a bit of shooting foxes in the face at the weekend, if the weathers good. Born into the top end of the 1%, Martin was both years ahead of his time and, inevitably, a man of it. Much as he desired and worked for a better world, he was also a prisoner of his circumstance.

He loved to hunt in the vast grounds of his estates in Galway, living a lifestyle of exceptional privilege obtained through the forced labour of thousands of others, maintained by a deeply exploitative, hostile, and cruel system of Empire. So, it's no surprise that discrepancy and hypocrisy characterize the ideology of the RSPCA.

Such ugly incongruity created fault lines running through the organizations philosophy which erupted in public in the 1970's, as factory farmers and fox hunters fought for control of the Board of Trustees with vegan ALF militants. The fact that such disparate groups could join - and subsequently clash - in the same organization is unsurprising given the conflicting passions of one of its principal founders.

Despite his contradictions, there's been no singular force for the animals quite like Richard Martins' in the Halls of Power since.

The RSPCA — where rescuing dogs and cats whilst eating chickens and pigs makes perfect sense.

POSTSCRIPT - I drank in the same pub as Trigger Martin, MP. Indeed, we trod the same floorboards, albeit 200 years apart. I lived for a time in Galway, his old Constituency, in the mid-1990's, and used to frequent the towns best public house - Naughton's Pub, in the heart of the old City. This building used to be Martin's City pad back in the day and I like to think his Spirit permeated down through the centuries as its where I and others planned our first forays into hunt sabotage as described elsewhere in this book. So powerful was his resonance through the Ages that I vaguely remember many a night being carried out of there by my comrades, filled with belief in the struggle and babbling incoherently.

And speaking of hunt sabotage...

The first recorded sabotage of a hunt ever was organised by **Fr. Eugene Sheehy**, a parish priest for the tiny village of Bruree in the west of Ireland.

Sheehy was a well-known Republican and head of the local chapter of the Land League, a pressure group that campaigned for Irish tenants' rights.

When local Landlord John Gubbins evicted three families from their homes in 1886, Fr. Sheehy organised the village GAA Hurling team to physically block access to their lands to Gubbins and his fellow foxhunters. They did so, and continued to do so throughout the winter, preventing any hunting that season. Gubbins sold his hunting horses the following year and disbanded the hunt. Total Success!

This makes it the first ever recorded act of hunt sabotage and the only known act of hunt sabotage organised by a priest. This is also the first time I've had something good to say about a 'Man of the Cloth'.

above left - **Fr. Eugene Sheehy**, *1841 – 1917, Worlds first Hunt Saboteur. Eamonn De Valera, - the maybe-son of the first hunter ever to experience hunt sabotage - was, for a time, one of Fr. Sheehy's altar boys, assisting him with Mass every Sunday as a youth.*

above right - **John Gubbins,** *1838-1906 – much-hated landlord, horse breeder, rumoured-to-be-dad of Eamonn de Valera, and the very first foxhunter to be sabotaged. Gubbins died a few years later, crushed by a falling horse. Stock images.*

Local folklore has it that one day following these events, Gubbins came across local women washing clothes in a river. Gubbins said to one that she should wash herself, as she was filthy. She retorted that no amount of soap and water would wash off the dirt that was on him. Well said that woman!

above – **GET OFF YOUR LAND!** - *a typical GAA hurling team from the 1880's. This is what faced down landlord* **John Gubbins** *and his crew whenever they attempted to foxhunt during the 1886/87 season in Bruree, Co. Limerick. The Hunt then disbanded, and Gubbins sold his horses. In short, a Total Success. Stock image.*

It's also rumoured that Gubbins was Eamonn De Valera's biological father. De Valera's mother is from Bruree and worked for a time as a maid in Gubbins's manor before she emigrated to New York and gave birth to Eamonn DeValera in 1882. DeValeras 'official' father, a Spanish artist named Juan DeValera, remains elusive. Archivists have not located any marriage certificate or any birth, baptismal, or death certificates (he reportedly died in 1885) for anyone of that name. Gubbins was known to have fathered quite a few illegitimate children and old Dev is thought by some to be one of them. So, the victim of the world's first hunt sabotage might also be the father of the father of Militant Conservative Irish Republicanism. Gubbins died at the young age of 46 when the horse he was rising fell on him as they attempted jumping over a fence. Wheels within wheels, my friend. Brings a tear to a glass eye....

DO I LOOK LIKE

YOUR MOTHER?

THE SECOND WAVE 1890-1922 -FIRST VEGETARIAN SOCIETIES AND RESTAURANTS; THIRD WAVE 1972-2014 — SECOND GENERATION OF VEGETARIAN SOCIETIES AND RESTAURANTS

above - *Glorious Anarchy* - *Illustration of **Richard 'Trigger" Martin** tackling a butcher at Smithfield Meat Market, London. Taking advantage of the uproar, captive cows break free and hungry street kids pilfer apples. Drawing by G. Cruikshank, circa 1840. Stock image.*

The historical record shows the existence of vegans in Ireland since at least the mid-1600's with "Linen" Cook. However, it was vegetarianism, not veganism, that was for a long time considered to be the logical end point of a cruelty-free diet and lifestyle. Public ignorance and industry propaganda combined to convince otherwise intelligent people that consuming another mammal's milk was somehow entirely beneficial, if not vital, for human health.

Dining out as a vegetarian, never mind as a vegan, in Ireland until very recently was a typically bland affair, even in the bigger cities. Chips and salad, with the anchovies taken out. The further out from the cities you went, the worse it got. In many places, all they offered vegetarians was a cold plate of Contempt (and maybe a salad). They couldn't even *pronounce* vegan properly. Nor could many vegans.

Typically, the very concept was regarded as a sort of anti-social, contrarian posture and a heretical slap in the face of orthodox Catholicism which holds human life as separately 'divine' with complete control over all that walks, crawls, swims, and flies. They call it Dominion and it has subtly perverted and polluted interactions with our non-human cousins for two thousand years, creating a species of snobs.

Challenging this embedded speciesist narrative required changing hearts and minds, a much more difficult task than even changing the Law. And the best way to a man's heart is through his stomach. Women, in my experience, tend to be easier to convince. Despite the odds, there now exists a thriving vegan cuisine culture in Ireland generally and much more so in the bigger cities. Evolving over a 130-year period, the scene has galvanised in acceptance, understanding and popularity over the last decade.

"The real, only and true vegetarians, are known as vegans, pronounced vague-an. These are the original nut-cutleters." Journalist Lucille Redmond tells it like it is in the Irish Times, April 15th, 1978.

The first purely vegan (pronounced *vee*-gun) restaurants didn't appear in Ireland until the short-lived 'Sseduced' opened in Temple Bar in 2013, 122 years after the first vegetarian restaurant opened its doors and a mere ten-minute walk away on Henry Street. Established by Brazillian-born Silvia Packter and serving up raw vegan organic food, Sseduced was the only such restaurant in the Country at the time.

Now, according to Happy Cow, Dublin has 13 dedicated vegan eateries, and most other cities and towns in Ireland have a decent range of quality vegan, or-vegan-friendly, eateries, too many to mention here.

"Free from the slightest suspicion of animal matter" advert for the Sunshine Dining rooms, Irish Times 28 Aug. 1891.

INSIDE THE RESTAURANTS AT THE HEART OF REVOLUTION - The first Vegetarian restaurant to open its doors in Ireland was in Belfast in 1890, established by Antrim man Leonard McCaughy. It gets a brief mention in a report written by the Belfast Vegetarian Society that year and not much more is known about it, including its name.

Next came Dublin's **Sunshine Vegetarian Dining Rooms** at 48 Grafton Street in 1891. A review of the restaurant notes good food and the place being "extremely patronised" since opening. *(Irish Times, 28 August 1891.)*

Established by the Dublin Vegetarian Society, the venture lasted about a year before closure. Again, little else is known about the restaurant except it offered "luncheons, dinners, special afternoon teas in delightfully pleasant rooms" (*The Irish Times, 28 August 1891*).

These humble beginnings were merely an *aperitif* for what was soon to come.

"Vegetarian food is the coming diet" advert for the Sunshine Dining Rooms, Irish Times, 2 Feb.1900.

THE COLLEGE RESTAURANT (VEGETARIAN) HOTEL,

BREAKFASTS, LUNCHEONS, DINNERS, AND TEAS.

Great Variety, Prompt Service, Lowest Prices.

OUR SIXPENNY AND TENPENNY TEAS ARE UNSURPASSED.

DELICIOUS DRINKS
From American Soda Fountain.

THE McCAUGHEY RESTAURANTS, LIMITED,
3 AND 4 COLLEGE STREET, DUBLIN.

above - *Advert for Dublin's first Vegetarian restaurant in the Irish Times 1900, established by Antrim man **Leonard McCaughey** in 1899. Stock image.*

In 1899, the **College Vegetarian Restaurant** was opened in Dublin by Leonard McCaughy and quickly proved to be popular amongst the city's small but growing vegetarian population. Intellectuals, playwrights, and poets mixed with Indian students, suffragettes, and revolutionaries over plates of vegetarian food. McCaughy had a chain of four vegetarian restaurants including in Belfast, Leeds, and Glasgow. The old Glasgow branch, situated on 6 Jamaica Street, is now a McDonalds.

The Dublin restaurant was a gathering spot for Sinn Fein and the IRA prior to the 1916 rising and provided revolutionary-minded Indian Nationals residing in Dublin a place to meet with Irish nationalists and discuss ridding both countries of the British Empire. Not to be outdone by the **Irish Farm Produce** café in the drama stakes, the Irish Times

(11 May 1912) reported that one of the restaurants chefs, a Mr Leon Cromblin, was discovered in the cellar of the premises with his throat badly cut and a razor by his side in an apparent suicide attempt. It's not known if he survived.

Offering "soups, savouries and sweets in great variety at popular prices", the Restaurant remained in business for a highly respectable 23 years, closing in January 1922.

POWER TO THE PEOPLE - A mere ten minutes' walk away at 21 Henry Street was the Irish Farm Produce vegetarian restaurant, run by feminist, Republican and vegetarian, Jenny Wise Power, wife of GAA founder John Wyse Power. Also established in 1899, it was another nexus of radicalism and food-centred politics.

Powers' broad political and social interests attracted a range of rebels and revolutionaries under one roof and the place quickly became a de facto rebel vegetarian canteen, meeting room and arms dump. Future Irish President Arthur Griffith met other revolutionaries there every day in the year prior to the Rising. Indeed, it was in this very establishment where 7 signatories of the Irish Declaration of Independence, the leaders of the upcoming Rising, put pen to paper, in 1916.

Both buildings, filled as they were with undesirable revolutionary types, had undercover cops, known as G-Men, permanently stationed across the street, patiently noting down who was frequenting them. One surviving G-man's notes writes of Thomas McDonagh, one of the leaders of the Rising and a lecturer in UCD, being seen entering the Restaurant with another Sinn Fein activist, carrying a "heavy bag" containing guns.

In other words, these restaurants were the complete opposite to an average McDonalds, where all the wankers are on the *inside*, while the radicals are standing outside, handing out "What's wrong with McDonalds" leaflets. (Coincidentally and perversely, this leaflet, which came in a small booklet form, was co-authored by Bob Lambert, himself an undercover cop who infiltrated an ALF arson cell in the 1980's.) The restaurant is even name checked in one of English literatures finest works no-one ever finishes, Ulysses. This fact only recently came to light because no-one had read that far into the book until now.

POWER TO THE PEOPLE – above- *Jenny Wyse Power,* *1858-1941 – feminist, republican,* *vegetarian and owner of the most exciting restaurant to have lunch in Europe at the* *time. So exciting it would've brought on indigestion in even the heartiest of stomachs.* *Outside of the Women's Rights movement, the Animal Rights movement, since its* *inception, is the only other freedom struggle to have had so many women involved in* *it, and at its vanguard. Stock image.*

The Irish Home Produce Café expanded its operations in early 1916, opening two bakeries in Leeson Street and Camden Street. A barely visible sign from this premises still exists painted on the gable end wall of Camden Street. The words "Homemade bread" remain, painted above a circular symbol, one of the 'made in Ireland' symbols used by the Irish Farm produce company.

During the Rising over Easter of 1916, Henry Street experienced looting and arson committed by both British soldiers and rebels, but the Restaurant survived and in fact was busy providing food to the rebels holed up round the corner in Dublin's General Post Office. Throughout the week of the Rising, vegetarian fayre was carried to the rebels through gaps made in the internal walls of buildings along the street to avoid British bullets.

Following the failed Uprising, the restaurant continued as the favourite haunt for the nations revolutionaries and was subject to raids by hostile, often drunk, Black and Tans, Winston Churchill's counter-revolutionary punishment squads. The restaurant would be smashed up as they searched for guns but was always soon back in business.

As the failed 1916 Rising gave way to the victorious War of Independence in 1922,

Jennie Wyse Power found herself and her restaurant the target of anti- Treaty IRA rebels. She had taken a pro-Treaty stance and fallen out with former comrades as a result. A Civil War ensued, pitting the newly formed Free State/Old IRA army against anti-Treaty IRA rebels. This new IRA (not to be confused with the new New IRA) frequently attacked the property of those they now opposed. The Camden Street bakery was partially burned in 1922 when two bombs were thrown through its windows.

One afternoon in 1923 two young men entered 21 Henry Street and sat down at a table, posing as regular customers. As tea was being served, they suddenly jumped up and took firebombs out of their coats, shouting their intent to burn the place down. They smashed their bombs on the ground and fled. The fire was quickly extinguished, and the attempt failed to do much damage.

Nevertheless, it seems the restaurant closed around this time, as Ms. Power became more involved in Free State politics, becoming a Senator in the new Irish Parliament. Jenny Wyse Power died in 1941.

The Irish Farm Produce Cafe remains one of Irelands, maybe Europe's, most exciting establishments to have had lunch. Filled as it was with rebels storing guns and bombs, Indian students plotting revolution with famous Irish playwrights and poets, regular raids by inebriated, shell-shocked British squaddies, arson attacks by IRA rebels, free deliveries to local revolutionary strongholds and "the best food in the easiest digestible form at an affordable cost", there was never a dull moment. The place constantly teetered on the verge of exploding, both literally and metaphorically. It's enough to give you indigestion. And to think Anthony Bourdain thought he was a hard nut for snorting coke from a frozen pig carcass.

"The most violent republicans I know are all vegetarians. Those who live on a diet of lentils and artichokes are always calling for the severed heads of kings. In the political sphere a diet of green beans seems dangerous". Oscar Wilde, 1887.

Ireland and India have experienced a similar historical trajectory since at least the 1850's - both counties, though vastly different in size, had undergone Empire-induced famine and revolution and both strived for Home Rule, or more, by the turn of the 1900's. The Breadbasket of Empire and the Duel in the Crown, as Ireland and India were respectively known, contained a growing native middle class who were vital for the smooth running of the System and by default knew also how to subvert the System.

So it was that when future Prime Minister of India V.V. Giri and a dozen more Indian law students arrived in Dublin in 1913, they entered a world of extreme poverty, strikes, lockouts and boiling, imminent revolution.

Giri and his compatriots studied for the Bar at Kings Inns and the recently established UCD, both hotbeds of Revolutionary Nationalism. They dined at one of the two Vegetarian restaurants in the city. Giri quickly developed his taste for revolutionary politics and anti-colonial struggle. He soon helped form the quaintly named Anarchical Society with a fellow Indian student and made strong links with the Irish Fenian agitators he met over vegetarian lunches.

ANARCHIAL IN THE UK – above - *V. V. Giri, 1894-1980, India's 4th Prime Minister, (1969-1974), comrade of Mahatma Gandhi and self-declared (vegetarian) Irishman. Giri was an activist in one of Irelands earliest anarchist groups, the quaintly named Anarchial Society. Composed mainly of Indian law students in Dublin, the Society learned from and gave support to the Irish revolutionary Republican movement immediately prior to the 1916 Rising. Giri was also a regular at the Irish Farm Produce restaurant where he first encountered the Fenians. They had a deep influence on him, as did socialist James Connelly. "When I am not an Indian, I am an Irishman" he boasted. When the Rising broke out, Giri was advised to flee back to India to avoid arrest by the Police who had been keeping a close eye on these student radicals. Stock image.*

In fact, one of Giri's Lecturers at UCD was none other than Thomas McDonagh, soon to be executed by the British following the failed 1916 Rising, and Giri was particularly impressed by raging righteous Socialist, James Connolly. The two became close friends and Giri was deeply influenced by Connolly's attitude and tactics. Giri and fellow Indian students often attended Irish Citizen Army meetings, further developing their own plans for forcing British withdrawal from India.

When Giri fled Dublin on orders from the Police following the Rising in 1916, he set up an Indian Transport and General Workers Union, modelled on the Irish Union, and organised one of the biggest strikes in India's history, complete with a lockout of the workers but in this case the workers won. He even set up a pacifist version of the Irish Volunteers called the Indian Volunteers. "I resolved to give a graphic account of these struggles to inspire our own people" he later wrote of his brief time in Dublin. Many years later, as the fourth President of India, he noted "When I am not an Indian, I am an Irishman". A *vegetarian* Irishman, of course.

"I met him the day before yesterday and he coming out of that Irish farm dairy John Wyse Nolan's wife has in Henry street with a jar of cream in his hand taking it home to his better half. She's well nourished, I tell you." James Joyce refers to the Irish Farm Produce restaurant in 'Ulysses' – the John Wyse Nolan referred to is John Wyse Power

The closure of both of Dublin's vegetarian restaurants in 1922 represent the end of an era, as other political issues came to the fore with the withdrawal of British Forces from Ireland and the establishment of the Irish Free State. This new State was not just broke, it was in massive debt to the Empire next door. The land-owning Anglo Protestant Ascendency had only agreed to hand back the land to the native Irish on condition they receive a massive pay out, crippling the new nation's economy from the get-go.

A long era of economic stagnation and emigration of the youth began, stifling the chances of a vibrant vegetarian culture.

True to form, Ireland's "Sixties" happened in the 1970's and it would be another 50 years before Dublin had another vegetarian restaurant. **Good Karma** on Strand St. opened its doors in 1972 and closed them again sometime in 1973, shut down by the Eastern Health Board for a minor violation of regulations, allegedly. At least one reviewer in the Irish Times reckoned it offered a "wholesome change from the stagnancy of Dublin's eating" (Elgy Gillespie, The Irish Times, 11 September 1972).

"There were numerous Garda raids, and the restaurant didn't last long"- journalist John Doyle remembers Good Karma, Irish Independent, 2005. It's unclear what the Gardai were looking for.

More vegetarian/wholefood eating establishments appeared in the city in the late 1970's, including **Munchies, Golden Dawn** and the **Supernatural Tearooms**. Golden Dawn was particularly well known and was a favourite of actor Gabriel Byrne and various music and media personalities until it was rebranded **Blazing Salads** by its owners Joe Fitzmaurice and family in 1982. It is still operating today as a takeaway vegetarian delicatessen in Drury Street. The Fitzmaurice's are considered trailblazers in Ireland's wholefood vegetarian community and have at least three cookbooks out. The vegetarian culinary scene in Ireland at this time seems to have been tied up with macrobiotic ideas as well, reflecting the hippie lifestyle of many, perhaps most, of Irelands contemporary vegetarians/vegans.

"Somehow you felt you were part of a social and gastronomic experiment" – Paolo Tullio, restaurant critic on Irelands vegetarian restaurants of the 1970's.

above - **MEET AND TWO VEG** - *diners enjoying the feast at the Golden Dawn restaurant, Dublin, circa 1978. Stock image.*

The **WELL FED Café**, part of the Dublin Resource Centre, began in 1983, also on Crow street, and was an award-winning worker-run cooperative specialising in cheap, nutritious vegetarian/vegan fayre. Lasting ten years, it gained iconic status amongst Dublin's anarcho punk and student communities.

Cornucopia Wholefood and Vegetarian Restaurant, the granddaddy of Dublin veggie restaurants, began trading on Wicklow Street in January 1986 and has been there ever since. It was established by Neil McCafferty (1952-1993) and Deirdre McCafferty, who is still the proprietor of the restaurant.

The Hare Krishna's got stuck into the action in the late 1980's when they opened a vegetarian restaurant, again on Crow Street but this was short lived. They went at it again ten years later, opening **Govinda's** restaurant at 4 Aungier Street in 1998. It is still in operation, as are two more Govinda's elsewhere in the city. Those guys must be praising the right god cos they're sure doing well.

I CAN'T BELIEVE ITS NOT BHUDDA- *Govinda* means 'cow finder' in Sanskrit and it's worth remembering that Hare Krishna's are most definitely not vegan. While they avoid meat, they consider cow milk and all associated products to be a gift from Krisna and absolutely intended for human consumption. They don't explain where the calf fits into gods plan..

HEY! HEY! WE'RE THE MONK-EES! – above - *Hare Krishna's in mid-flow. These guys have managed to sustain several vegetarian restaurants in central Dublin since the 1980's. Specialising in cheap nutritious vegan slop and mandatory background chanting, what's not to like, apart from the background chanting? The Hare Krisna's refer to themselves as prasadivores, not vegetarians. Prasad is food that has been sanctioned by Krisna and this very much includes dairy. Milk, they state is "designed by God for humans and not just the calf."This inevitabley begs the question – just what animal is human breast milk for? They do usually cater for vegans though. They need the money for haircuts and bongo drums. Stock image.*

CRANKS, from the UK, opened a Dublin branch in Westmoreland Street in 1989 and operated for a few years before closing and leaving a solitary sit-down vegetarian restaurant in the city throughout the 1990's, **Juice**. Popular throughout its many years of service, Juice closed in 2011. Other vegetarian restaurants in Dublin from the 1980's include **Bananas, Harvest**, **Second Nature**, and **Rays** but little is available online about them.

above - *Another famous culinary institution, Dublin's **Cornucopia** restaurant on Wicklow St., has been serving Irelands vegetarian and vegan population since 1986. Stock image.*

21

Outside of Dublin, options for quality vegetarian/vegan dining were usually sparse and, shall we say, unimaginative, hostile even.

Thankfully my hometown had, and still has, the gourmet **Paradiso Café/Restaurant** and the **Quay Co-op**, on Sullivan's Quay in central Cork City, a three-story behemoth including a large health food store and multi-level dining rooms, open both day and night. In operation since 1982, the Co-op has been a haven for Cork's artists, outcasts, and gastronomic misfits. Good vegan and vegetarian shop , an affordable restaurant alongside a radical bookshop and meeting room, the Co-op has been at the centre of Ireland's social progress movements over the years.

*above - Corks long standing HQ of Hope and Tower of Taste, the **Quay Co-op**. Employing over 60 people and now with branches in Carrigaline and Ballincollig, the Quay Co-op has been a cornerstone of alternative politics and veg*n food in Cork for over 40 years. The Co-op is also now directly working with **Dublin's Food Co-op**, a vegetarian/ vegan food buying Co-operative and shop in operation since the mid-1980's with over 2000 members. "People sometimes crossed to the other side of the street to avoid it when passing the building on Sullivans Quay" observed Liz Dunphy on the early days of the Quay Co-ops existence. Irish Examiner, 17 Sept. 2021. Stock image.*

Employing over 60 people and now with branches in Carrigaline and Ballincollig and Online, the Quay Co-op has been a cornerstone of alternative politics and food in Cork for over 40 years. It's interesting to note the original campaigns associated with the early Quay Co-op - gay rights, access to abortion, rights to divorce and contraception, have all been won. Early in its existence the Quay Co-op was a magnet for paranoid Special Branch undercover police who kept a close eye on the type of books and magazines on sale there. A report in the Evening Echo from April 9th, 1984, describes a meeting between the local Garda Superintendent and the Co-ops management to discuss a book found by plainclothes police in the Co-op that "a portion of which related to timing devices". The book –a dry 1955 text on telephones – was enough to justify a subsequent raid and interrogation from Police, who eventually decided the Co-op is "only engaged in lawful activities".

The Co-op is also now directly working with **Dublin's Food Co-op**, a vegetarian/vegan food buying co-operative and shop in operation since the mid-1980's and with over 2000 members.

Alongside the anarcho-punk collective **Warzone's 'Giro's Cafe'** in central Belfast, the Quay Co-op most resembles the revolutionary spirit of the vegetarian restaurants of 1920's Dublin.

Opened by Warzone in 1984, Giros provided a space for people on both sides of the conflict to meet, unique for Belfast in the 1980's.

Located in the city centre, the cafe was surrounded by streets lined with sandbags and British soldiers. Central Belfast was a heavily fortified cultural desert due to bombings and sectarian divisions. CCTV was everywhere (unusual for the time) and army helicopters constantly hovered in the skies above.

Frequented largely by Belfast's significant punk and art student communities, Giro's grew and expanded until the Warzone Collective folded in 2003.

Giros reopened in 2009 and continued its cafe and gig operations until folding again in 2018. The Warzone Collective still exists and maybe Giros part 3 will emerge someday.

Above – *inside Giro's cafe, central Belfast. Circa 1990. Giros was the vegetarian/ vegan cafe operated by the anarcho punk collective **Warzone.** Stock image.*

Opening in 1984, Giros provided a space for people on both sides of the conflict to meet, unique for Belfast in the 1980's.

Located in the city centre, the cafe was surrounded by streets lined with sandbags and British soldiers. Central Belfast was a cultural desert at the time due to bombings and sectarian divisions. Unusual for the era, CCTV was everywhere and army helicopters often hovered in the skies above.

Frequented largely by Belfast's significant punk and student communities, Giro's grew and expanded until the Warzone Collective folded in 2003.

Giros reopened in 2009 and continued its cafe and gig operations until folding again in 2018. The Warzone Collective still exists and maybe Giros part 3 will emerge someday. Establishments like Giros, the Quay Co-Op and the Food Cooperative most closely resemble the revolutionary flavour of Dublin's earliest vegetarian restaurants like the Farm Produce Café.

TWO'S COMPANY / ONE'S A CROWD - The world's first Vegetarian Society was formed in England, in 1847. In 1888 the Society split when the London Branch of the Vegetarian Society fell out with the rest of the movement. The London branch wanted to include raw food ideas into the Societies philosophy and formed their own breakaway faction when this was deemed too radical by everyone else. There now existed the London Vegetarian Society, of whom Mahatma Gandhi was a member, and the rest of the organisation who became known as the Manchester Vegetarian Society. Both released seperate publications and organised meetings to spread the message but would not re-amalgamate until 1969, forming the current-day Vegetarian Society of the United Kingdom.

Meanwhile, Ireland in 1847 did not have a Vegetarian Society. In fact, Ireland in 1847 saw Society in general in freefall. That year - Black '47 - was the third consecutive year that the potato crop had succumbed to blight and millions starved. Whole regions of the Country resembled a post-apocalyptic scene of smashed houses and mass grave pits, of dead and dying families lying in freezing, barren fields, of cartloads of fresh food being marched out of the Country by the soldiers of Empire and of fleets of coffin ships carrying the half dead and half crazed millions away from a living nightmare of the Empires making.

above – **Moira Henry,** *19??-1997 (being pointed out) as one of the delegates at the 11th International Vegetarian Union World Vegetarian Congress ,1947. Stonehouse, England. Stock image.*

Described by the Irish Press in 1949 as "the only Vegan in Ireland", Moira was elected Secretary of the newly formed Dublin Vegetarian Society in 1947.This organisation had 33 members, though the Society reckoned there were "about 104" vegetarians in the Republic (*source* An Irishman's Diary, 5 March 1951). By 1955 the Societies numbers had ballooned to 55.

"There are no figures for the number of vegetarians in Ireland, since most of them are ragged individuals who wouldn't be seen dead on a plate in a society or association of any sort." Lucile Redmond, Irish Times, April 15, 1978.

YOU WAIT ALL CENTURY FOR A VEGETARIAN SOCIETY AND THEN THREE COME AT ONCE - The first Vegetarian Society in Ireland was stated in Belfast around 1878. They established as a branch of the Manchester Vegetarian Society and folded less than two years later. A decade later Dublin activists set up the Dublin Vegetarian Society in 1890, again as a branch of the Manchester (i.e., British) Vegetarian society as Ireland North and South was then part of the British Empire. The Society managed to establish the Sunshine Vegetarian Restaurant the next year, the first of its kind outside of Belfast.

Also in 1890, the London Vegetarian Society helped establish another Vegetarian Society in Belfast. There also existed an Irish Vegetarian Union group, bringing to three the number of Vegetarian Societies in the country at the turn of the 20th century. All three Societies were essentially independent and each hosted public meetings, food tasting and distributed literature. Information on their histories is short but it seems the movement overall was small in number and considered at best an eccentricity by the general populace. All of these organisations appear to have died out during World War One. The mid-twentieth century was a low point for animal concerns in Ireland. Global war, a stagnant economy and tensions with Northern Ireland and the UK dominated public and political discourse. However, despite this, the Dublin Vegetarian Society was formed in 1949 and lasted into the 1960's. This group was tiny, with a few dozen members, but they kept the flame alive. The Society maintained contact with the International Vegetarian Union, sending delegates (usually **Moira Henry** – see below) to their annual Conferences, but otherwise appear to have had negligible impact on Irish eating habits or opinions.

"Vegetarianism in those days was regarded as cranky and perverse"- R.G. writing in the Irish Press, 1997.

The history of Veganism in Ireland in the mid-20th Century can best be told through the lives of the few brave and enlightened individuals who devoted their lives to furthering the Cause against an indifferent and often bemused populace. Up until quite recently no formal vegan organisations existed here and after Robert Cooks death in 1726 the record on vegans in Ireland is silent until the sterling Ms. Moira Henry over two hundred years later in the 1930's.

"A Vegan is a Super-Vegetarian"- Irish Press 26/02/1949, by way of explanation.

 Described by the Irish Press in 1949 as "the only Vegan in Ireland", and "Vegan No.1", Dubliner Moira Henry was a noted journalist and dressmaker as well as a life-long campaigner for animal rights. Usually wearing striking make-up and her own clothing (very punk), Moira became vegetarian "on 15 March 1934 then vegan a few years later." Not surprisingly, this was a most unusual decision to make in Ireland in the 1930's. Societies endorsement of animal cruelty weighed heavily on Moira's shoulders.

Moira was elected Secretary of the newly formed Dublin Vegetarian Society in 1947. This organisation had 33 members, though the Society reckoned there were "about 104" vegetarians in the Republic (An Irishman's Diary, 5 March 1951). By 1955 the Society's numbers had increased to 55. Moira was a regular attendee at the annual International Vegetarian Unions' gatherings in the UK and Secretary General for the Irish Union Against Vivisection. Life must have been tough for Moira, living in a society where indifference to animal suffering was so entrenched in almost everyone else's minds, a society where concern for animals well being was considered eccentric at best, and insane by many. A true revolutionary.

Moira died in 1997.

"An irreplaceable person for whom the world was too distressing a place"- R.G. writing about Moira Henry in the Irish Press, 1997.

The late 1970's saw a re-emergence of civil initiatives promoting vegetarianism. In 1978 Tolkien enthusiast and Esperanto speaker Christopher Fettes revamped the Vegetarian Society of Ireland and it continued the outreach work of its predecessors (in English, not Esperanto or Elvish).

This Society seems to be dormant, if not extinguished, in 2023 at time of writing. Their website references stuff 'coming up' in 2018 and they haven't published their quarterly magazine since 2014. Their latest drop on YouTube was on World Vegetarian Day in 2018 when they held a public meeting and had three guests on their Panel, all of whom are vegan. Has the Irish Vegetarian movement been outpaced by the surging Vegan movement perhaps?

above - **Jack McClelland,** 1924-1996**,** *receiving his trophy for swimming the 7 miles (10K) from Tory Island to Donegal, 1968. It took him six hours in cold, choppy conditions. Jack refused to smear his body in the customary goose fat as insulation from the freezing seas. I'd expected a bigger trophy if I were him. image from RTE archives.*

Another noteworthy vegan personality is Jack McClelland (1922-1979), Irelands (perhaps the Worlds) first vegan Ultra athlete. Champion swimmer, professional-level footballer, weightlifter, and wrestler (the 'Belfast Bulldog'), Jack was a leading activist with the UK Vegan Society and the Ulster Vegetarian Society throughout the 1940's and 50's. He also owned a chain of health food stores in Ireland, enabling the Country's embryonic vegan movement to survive and thrive.

McClelland was best known as a long-distance swimmer and famously swam the 10K distance from Rathlin Island to the mainland as well as Dingle Bay (20k) and, in 1963, Galway Bay (30k). In fact, more people turned out to see Jack swim Galway Bay than showed up for John F. Kennedy's visit to Galway a few weeks earlier. He also swam the English Channel in 1956 and the 9 miles between Tory Island and the Irish mainland in 1968.

Bear in mind Jack refused to use the traditional goose fat that open water swimmers usually apply all over their body to keep out the freezing cold. The seas that surround Ireland are so cold that, in winter at least, just running in-and-out for a quick dip is considered totally hardcore and/or a bit mad. BRRRR!

My hand feels cold from just writing about it.

Jack, from the Protestant community of Northern Ireland, received criticism when 'the Troubles' began in 1969 by suggesting the outbreak of inter-communal violence in Belfast was partly due to the meat-and-dairy-heavy diet of the Irish. Violence against farm animals was generating violence between people, he proposed.

What he failed to explain was why violence was suddenly breaking out now, and only in one part of one island. The diet elsewhere was the same, so why not the violence? It was a fairly ignorant thing to say, and flies in the face of the vegetarian background of the militant republican movement in Dublin in the early 20th century. It also says a lot more about his relatively privileged place in the Protestant-dominated Northern Ireland of the time, perhaps blinding him to the reality of poverty as experienced by disenfranchised Catholics.

However, he made huge contributions to the vegan movement in Ireland and was a truly unique figure given the length and breadth of his activities. I had never even heard of the guy until I read about him in **Corey Lee Wrenn's** wonderful 'other book about the Irish animal rights movement', '**Animals in Irish Society**", published in 2021. He stands out in so many ways, but his legacy has been neglected. Outside of the animal rights milieu, the few brief mentions about him online focus only on his (many) sporting achievements. They don't say anything about his veganism and animal advocacy. There should be statues of the fella in his swimming trunks at beaches and outside vegan cafes up and down the country, not just a few bland lines tucked away in an obscure sporting website.

CONTEMPORARY IRELAND.

As noted, veganism and concern for animals generally have come to the fore in Ireland in the last decade or so. The prevalence of nature's destruction caused by animal agriculture makes the issue impossible to ignore. Veganism has stepped out of the shadows and is now more accepted and catered for than ever before. This *movement of movements* for animal rights is in a new wave on its historical trajectory. Social Media has largely replaced Direct Action as a means to shift the dial on our behaviour toward other animal species. Governments, including Irelands, have finally begun to consider challenging the free ride given to animal agriculture by increasing taxes.

People like actress Evanna Lynch, author Holly White, twin brothers the Happy Pear, super-wrestler Becky Lynch and many others have helped to normalise and popularise veganism to an unprecedented degree. No- one, least of all the vegan community, saw this coming.

above – *staple vegan fast food in the olden days – crisp sangwitches and sosmix sossiddges. Stock images.*

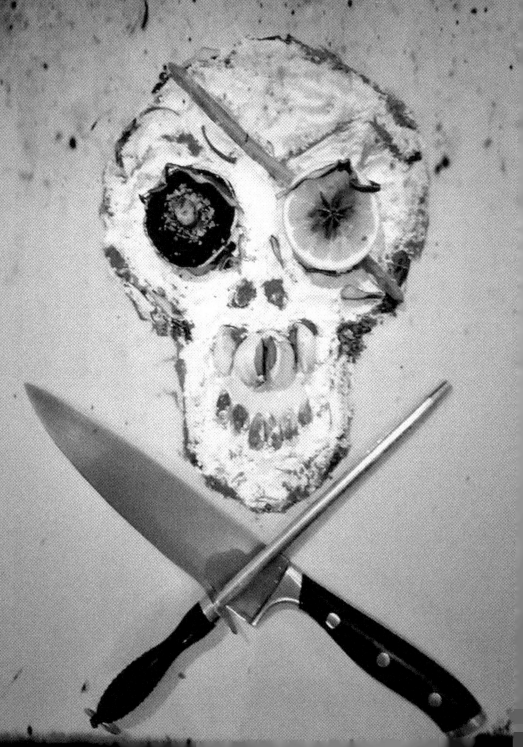

CHAPTER THREE - ANGER IS AN ENERGY - THE ORIGINS AND RISE OF THE HUNT SABOTEURS / THE ANIMAL LIBERATION FRONT / ANARCHO PUNK : THE FOURTH WAVE (1982-2010-ISH)

"Let ten men meet who are resolved on the lightning of violence. From that moment on despair ends and tactics begin" Raoul Vaneigum, anarchist poet.

There has been a thin but constant thread of actions against violence against animals on this Island since the advent of the Animal Liberation Front in Ireland in 1982. Hundreds of direct actions are recorded in small articles in regional, and sometimes national, Irish newspapers. When combined into a coherent narrative and timeline, they describe a history of regular and persistent acts of sabotage and animal rescue that would otherwise fade into historical oblivion. These actions represent a foot-in-the-door opening on the issue of violence against animals, a vital and vocal genesis of active defence of sentient life on this island.

The ALF – both here and globally - reached it's peak in the 1990's and has slowly receded from the socio/political landscape since around 2010. Periodic actions are still claimed by the group but nothing on the scale of 20-30 years ago. Massive State repression (particularly in the UK and the USA) combined with the rapid spread of CCTV and other surveillance everywhere have supressed the direct-action movement for animals, forcing new tactics to be employed such as the Open Rescue method of Meat the Victims, Animal Rebellion and Direct Action Everywhere.

"The point of it fundamentally was to create a shock wave" - anonymous ALF activist.

above - *The **Animal Liberation Front – helping animals out since 1976.** Barry Horne and anonymous other with some of the 82 dogs they rescued from Interfauna vivisection laboratory, Cambridge, UK, March 17 (St. Patricks Day!) 1990. source ALF online archive.*

ORIGINS - The Animal Liberation Front was started in the UK by **Ronnie Lee,** a trainee solicitor from Luton, when he got released from prison in 1976. It grew out of the **Band of Mercy** (BoM), which itself was a secretive offshoot of the **Hunt Saboteurs Association** (HSA).

The Hunt Saboteurs Association was formed in 1962 in Devon, southern England, initially as an informal direct-action wing of the **League Against Cruel Sports (LACS)**. LACS had by his point been campaigning legally for decades with limited success – they had helped get otters and badgers protected by law in 1978 and 1992 respectively. By and large they kept on the 'right side' of the Law because they assumed this position would be reciprocated by the Hunting fraternity if and when hunting got banned. Fair's fair and the Law's the Law and all that. What they discovered, when hunting was finally outlawed in 2004, was that Hunts continued to hunt with relative impunity. Unlike their frequent massive presence at Hunts when it was legal, Police were nowhere to be seen since the Ban. It's been up to the HSA, RSPCA and a wiser LACS to monitor Hunts. Drones and phones are now the preferred weapon of the anti-hunt movement, gathering evidence of law-breaking to be used as evidence in Court.

Since the Ban there have been almost 600 successful prosecutions.

Appetite for Destruction

above - **ALF OG** -UK born, Irish citizen and co-founder of the Animal Liberation Front **Ronnie Lee**. Stock image.

Beginning in January 1964, HSA activists would go into the hunting ground and directly interfere with the hunting process in the hope of saving the quarry, usually a fox, hare or stag. Using voice and horn-calls that mimicked the hunters', or simply distracting the hounds by feeding them loads of meat (!) and setting off flares and smoke bombs, the Saboteurs were devastatingly effective. Confusion reigned, making hunting impossible.

When faced with the inevitable violent reaction from hunters and their supporters, the early activists had two responses – run away or curl up into a ball and hope for the best. Misled by Gandhian pacifist theory, they hoped their principled victimhood would nurture sympathy from the public and politicians, and maybe even amongst the hunting fraternity.

This soon expanded to include making written notes of time and place and descriptions of who attacked you, all to present to a grateful police force eager to bring any aggressors to justice. When Saboteurs realised the Police were not just apathetic but often actively hostile to their cause, an impasse was reached – either succumb to the constant violence and go home via the hospital, or step things up a gear or two and match fire with fire.

By the mid 1970's, Ronnie Lee and fellow Hunt Saboteurs based around North London decided enough was enough and a new, dramatically different tactic was instigated – from now on, any aggression shown against the Sabs would be met by an immediate swarm of counter-violence.

"As soon as they laid the slightest finger on anyone, we'd attack" Lee said, "We wouldn't stand for any of it." On one occasion, "one of the hunters hit one of the hunt sabs and an all-out fight broke out because we fought back against him." When it was over, the Saboteurs were victorious, and a half dozen hunters lay in a ditch writhing in pain.

"As soon as they laid the slightest finger on anyone, we'd attack"- Hunt Saboteur Ronnie Lee.

The Hunting fraternity's response to this escalation was to notch things up another rung. Raymond Brooks-Ward, Master of the Enfield Chase Hunt and a show jumping commentator on the BBC, formed the **Hunt Protection Squad** – local thugs employed to take on the Sabs. They quickly met their match when Lee gathered a squad of Saboteurs who were proficient in karate for a 'regional hit' on the Enfield Chase FoxHunt. As three carloads of hunt Sabs approached the hunt one Saturday morning, the Hunt Protection Squad ran at their vehicles and pulled open the doors of the leading car - "a boot came flying out and kicked him in the face "says Lee, "they (the karate sabs) were so brilliant. As soon as they started on one guy, all the others ran away because they thought 'shit these guys are going to kill us."'

Surprisingly their stance was initially rejected by the HSA leadership and most other Sab groups refused to work with them.

above - ***FIGHT OR FLIGHT? FIGHT AND FLIGHT****...December 1997, Bishops Waltham, Hampshire, UK, about 100 hunt saboteurs descend on the Hursley and Hambledon Hunt. Armed with baseball bats, iron bars and staves, they immediately begin to smash all and any vehicle belonging to the Hunt and their supporters. Anyone who tried to stop them was attacked and three hunters were hospitalised. Dozens of hunters' vehicles were badly damaged. This attack was in retaliation for sustained aggression and violence, including sexual assault and numerous death threats, against saboteurs by this Hunt in the recent past. The violence was condemned by the HSA. Police arrested 42 sabs as they fled the area following the attack. All charges were later dropped and violence from the Hursley and Hambledon Hunt quickly waned after their thrashing.*

"The violence was tremendous. Everything in sight was obliterated. It looked like a bomb had gone off" said Gamekeeper Phillip Mansbridge, witness to the attack. "The SAS would have been proud of the way it had been planned" he added.

*Stock image.*above - ***a mink hunter enters the marketplace of ideas***. *Northants, UK, 1991. from HOWL#47. Talking, then shouting, then pointing, then throwing rocks - the inevitable conclusion of debating with a hunter. source HSA archive.*

However, this shift was a pivotal moment in the history of the movement. Over time, most hunt Saboteurs accepted the necessity of active self-defence. A tactic developed whereby, if a group of Sabs were attacked anywhere in the country, the following week several other nearby Sab groups would descend on that hunt for a day of very intense sabotage. These were known as 'Regional hits' and proved highly effective in suppressing violence from the hunting fraternity. Where necessary, a much bigger 'National hit' would be arranged. The hunt might have 200-plus Sabs turn up, making hunting impossible and often leading to violence.

Out of this situation the **Hunt Retribution Squad** formed to go on the offensive against certain Hunts that were felt to be out of control in their aggression against saboteurs. Not content with bringing the concept of assertive self-protection into the movement, Lee and a half-dozen other Sab's formed a secret offshoot of the HSA named the Band of Mercy (BoM), after a 19th Century anti-vivisection society of the same name.

Starting in the autumn of 1973, the BoM's specialty was to vandalize vehicles and property owned by members of the Hunt, either on their property or when their vehicles were parked in quiet country lanes as their owners hunted. Vehicles belonging to the Vale of Aylesbury Foxhunt and other nearby hunts regularly had their vehicle tyres slashed, windscreens broken, and engines ruined.

Their range of targets expanded quickly and within a few years the Band of Mercy were burning down vivisection laboratories and boats used for seal culling until the main two activists in the group -Lee and a fellow hunt sab named Cliff Goodman - were caught preparing to firebomb the Oxford Laboratory Animal Colonies building in Bicester, which bred animals for the vivisection industry. They both received 3-year prison terms, making them the world's first animal rights prisoners. Lee was served further charges whilst in prison for his involvement with a group called British Withdrawal from Northern Ireland Campaign. Lee, whose mother was Irish, was familiar with Ireland, having gone there for many a family holiday just as the 'Troubles' were getting going. Politically anti-Imperialist, Lee had been going round various military bases in England handing out leaflets titled 'Some Information for Discontented Soldiers'. These leaflets informed squaddies on how they could leave the army if they were unhappy at the prospect of being "part of the British occupation of the North of Ireland". After a pivotal 51-day trial, Lee and 13 others were acquitted in the Old Bailey of all charges of Incitement to Disaffection.

Lee and Goodman were paroled after serving 12 months of their sentence. Upon release, Cliff Goodman hung up his balaclava and retired from activism. He also told the police everything they wanted to know, thereby also becoming the first snitch in the animal rights movement. Not so for Ronnie Lee, however.

Along with a few dozen others, Lee established the Animal Liberation Front within months of his release. The ALF's first action was in the summer of 1976 with a raid on the Pfizer's laboratory in Kent. Three pregnant beagles were rescued who went on to have 13 pups between them.

"Thou shalt not be a victim, thou shalt not be a perpetrator. Above all, thou shalt not be a bystander"- Yehuda Bauer, Holocaust historian.

WE'RE NUMBER ONE - *A full 80 or so years before Crass released their first EP and kickstarted the whole anarcho punk movement, a more gentle, less expletive-ridden scene arose called the Band of Mercy (BoM). The BoM were an offshoot of the RSPCA and was aimed at children and adolescents. The BoM held weekly meetings in their locale, gathering the youth to sing songs in praise of kindness toward animals and declare their willingness to defend them when required. The little rascals were also given to breaking hunters' guns and rescuing animals destined for vivisection. This was at a time when vivisection was completely unregulated and could be performed by anyone with a scalpel and a hammer. Stock image.*

The Bands were huge in Britain and the USA at the turn of the 20th century - the US had 27,000 chapters and a full 3% of United States citizens aged between 5 and 15 were signed up.

Each member pledged to do **"all in our power to protect animals from cruel usage, and to promote as far as we can their humane treatment."**

Lyrics from their songs could be quite militant and often soaked in religious references as reflected the times they were written in .Some lyrics could have come straight from a Conflict song - "Stand by your conscience, your honour, your faith, / Stand like a hero and battle till death" ; "Marshall forth the Bands of Mercy o'er all the Earth , till war oppression and hatred cease, In the reign of liberty love and peace".

Things rapidly escalated from there. Over the next 6 years, the ALF spread all over Great Britain, overseas to the USA and across continental Europe and Ireland.

A detailed history of the UK ALF is told in Keith Mann's excellent book 'Dusk till Dawn" and elsewhere, so I won't go into too much detail, but it is important to note a few things about the ALF mindset and strategy to best understand their tactics.

It's important to understand the ALF are not particularly interested in the public's perception of them. They do not depend on the support of the general public to exist, unlike Greenpeace or the RSPCA. This is what separates them from animal welfare and conservationist groups.

As most of the public and the economic system are deeply embedded in our species exploitation of the animal kingdom, their reactions to ALF actions cannot be the barometer of what is considered acceptable in the pursuit of animal rights. To the ALF and others, the question is not what people will think about this or that action. Rather, the question is - what would the animals want us to do for them? Or more pertinently still – what would I want to see happen if I were in the animal's situation? Seen from this point of view, the ALF have been a remarkably and consistently restrained force.

The ALF are against all violence against any living sentient creature, humans included. Some actions may cause temporary upset and chaos in society or upon certain individuals or Corporations but never physical violence. Shock and Awe, not Shoot and Kill. This is what separates them from "militant" groups. Others, of course, insist the ALF and associates are nothing *but* terrorists, putting their own cause 'back by years'. The fact of the matter, however, is that if the previous century of entirely peaceful and legal attempts at change had been effective, the Direct Action wing of the movement would never have arisen. All successful movements of liberation, from the slaves to women to the working classes, have required a moderate and radical flank in order to be effective. Liberation for animals is no different.

A MESSAGE FROM
THE 'BAND OF MERCY'

WE ARE RESPONSIBLE
FOR THE BLAZES AT
THE HOECHST RESEARCH
LABORATORY AT WALTON
[SATURDAY 11TH + SUNDAY
18TH NOVEMBER]
THE BUILDING WAS SET
FIRE TO IN AN EFFORT
TO PREVENT THE TORTURE
AND MURDER OF OUR
ANIMAL BROTHERS +
SISTERS BY EVIL
EXPERIMENTS
WE ARE A NONVIOLENT
GUERILLA ORGANISATION
DEDICATED TO THE
LIBERATION OF ANIMALS
FROM ALL FORMS OF
CRUELTY AND PERSECUTION
AT THE HANDS OF MANKIND

OUR ACTIONS WILL
CONTINUE UNTIL OUR
AIMS ARE ACHIEVED

ABOVE - The letter that the Band of
Mercy sent to the press,
claiming responsibility for
the arson attacks.

continued over.............

"It is a war without killing but a war, nonetheless. To advocate anything less than war when faced with the brutal tyranny of the human race over all other creatures is a form of treachery against the animals" UK Animal Liberation Front.

above -the first ever communique in 1973 from the first ever organised group of people taking sustained direct action on behalf of animals. The Band of Mercy, an informal off-shoot of the Hunt Saboteurs Association, were the precursor to the Animal Liberation Front. The significance of this message, being the first of its kind and widely circulated in the media, cannot be overstated in the history of struggle against violence against animals. Source - ALF SG newsletter #17, p.17/18.

THE RISE OF THE ANIMAL LIBERATION FRONT IN IRELAND - Throughout the 1970's,80's and 90's, the Statelet of Northern Ireland was, in the words of British Intelligence historian Stephen Dorril, the *"most surveyed 'country' in the world. Every citizen, probably, had a file, every household was under surveillance down to the most minute detail"*. This is no exaggeration. Given the small and compact nature of the Six Counties, it was quite easy for the British State to build up a database of everything they wanted to know on everyone who lived there. Communities were surrounded by tall army towers that monitored every street and doorway. Microphones were hidden in the most unlikely of places to eavesdrop on conversations – on buses, in walls and gardens, in pubs and clubs. Armed roadblocks popped up randomly. Special powers gave the police authority to search everything, everyone and everywhere at any time. Northern Ireland was practically a petri dish for experiments in total State surveillance and counter-insurgency techniques. A complex and opaque network of State operatives policed and surveyed the population relentlessly. The RUC, the British Army, the SAS, MI5, the Special Reconnaissance Unit, the UVF, the UDA, the LVF, the B-Specials, the Force Research Unit, Psychological Operations Unit (Black, Grey and White), Information Policy Unit- and these are the ones we know about, 15 separate institutions, all with eyes and ears on the public like a multi-eyed Sauron looming over the clouds. Running around at night-time with a balaclava on was seriously detrimental to your health, whatever the cause.

A highly gerrymandered and exclusive electoral system topped it all off as *the* perfect apartheid police State, one to model all others on.

It was, in the words of Liberal MP John Morley from 1902 *"the best machine that has ever been invented for governing a country against its will".*

Beat that, Kim Jong-un.

"We are a non-violent guerrilla organisation dedicated to the liberation of animals from all forms of cruelty and persecution at the hands of mankind" from the first ever communique from the Band of Mercy, 1973.

Despite this, the North of Ireland saw the first ALF actions in Ireland, and throughout the 1980's and 90's the activists there were easily the most prolific and belligerent.

CANCEL CULTURE - The first mention of animal liberation in Ireland took place in 1964 at Crebilly Coursing Grounds in Co. Antrim. Person's unknown cut a large hole in the fence of the compound holding the hares. The Coursers arrived for their fun the next day and discovered an empty compound and a damaged fence. The Club had to cancel its meet.

No group ever claimed the action and Police (the RUC) speculated that it was 'pranksters or someone opposed to blood sports'.

A lull of 18 years was broken in 1982 when two fur shops in Belfast city centre had their windows smashed three times over a 5-week period and a mink farm just outside the city was daubed with graffiti. All actions were claimed by the Animal Liberation Front and heralded their first appearance in Ireland.

This cell struck again a year later when they paid a nocturnal visit to a factory 'farm' in Castlereagh, Belfast. Eight hens were rescued, and farm machinery was damaged.

Also in 1982, an incident occurred which again may or may not have been the work of animal activists - 3 masked men, one wielding a shotgun, burst into the security guards' room at Whitford Polo Grounds in Wexford. They immediately overpowered the lone security guard, tied him up and then set all the hares free from the compound they were being held for the following days Coursing event. No group ever claimed the action and other than Richard Martin MP, animal activists tend not to use guns. It may have been a rival Coursing club, but they typically steal hares, not set them free. There was an active ALF cell in Wexford around this time so perhaps it was their work. Either way, the hare's were happy.

Northern Irelands Crebilly Coursing Club again faced the wrath of the animal rights community when dozens of activists blockaded the entrance to the Club in November 1984.The RUC had to forcibly remove people, delaying the event, and garnering much media attention. Civil disobedience in the name of animals was a novelty and the Press were fascinated.

The next month saw a repeat performance at Crebilly. Extra police had been drafted in to protect the Club and its activities. Despite RUC numbers and experience at crowd control, a 100-strong group from the student-based Anti-Blood Sports Society led a surge through police lines and blockaded the Clubs entrance. Two people were arrested, and the event eventually went ahead. Both actions garnered a lot of publicity and reflected the younger, more dynamic influx of campaigners to the movement.

A few nights later the ALF raided a Coursing Club in nearby Dungannon on two consecutive nights. They set all 40 hares free the first night and returned 24 hours later to tear down half the fencing around the now-empty enclosure. Just to make sure.

Hare Coursing was essentially banned in Northern Ireland in 2002, with a formal prohibition coming into law in 2011. Despite massive public opposition, Park Hare Coursing remains legal in the Irish Republic.

Successful actions in Great Britain were often an inspiration for activists in Ireland. Take the Mars Bar poisoning hoax for example.

The Mars corporation had been cynically funding "research" on rhesus monkeys into tooth decay. This involved feeding the monkeys a high sugar diet (like mars bars) to destroy their teeth, then trying out various "cures" (cure no.1 – don't eat mars bars). When this research came to light, the animal rights community was outraged.

THE MOUSE THAT ROARED - Where a more mainstream animal rights organization might spend years and millions on slowly building public awareness, pleading with industry figures, and lobbying politicians to intervene – with perhaps little or no success- the ALF went straight for the jugular.

A MARS A DAY? HOW ABOUT NO MARS IN TEN DAYS? - In November 1984, two Mars Bars were delivered to the BBC and the Mirror newspaper. Both bars of confectionary contained small doses of Alphakil rat poison with a letter claiming many more poisoned Mars Bars were in public circulation. Dozens of Mars Bars with a large "**X**" drawn on the wrapper started showing up on shelves in shops all over Britain. When opened, the Bars contained warning letters similar to those received by the media.

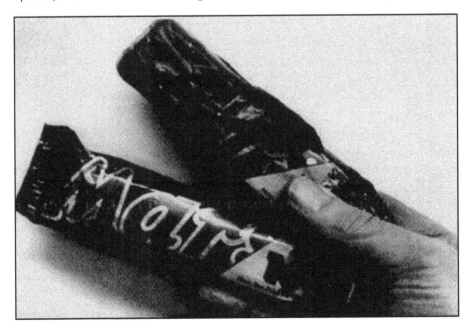

above - *the only two poisoned Mars Bars were these two that were sent into the media. Stock image.*

A CONFEDERACY OF DUNCES - The media, then the public, followed by the State, blew up. The tabloids went to town on the story, with dubious reports of people feeling nauseous after eating a Mars Bar. Sales of the product dropped to zero for an entire ten days and took *ten weeks* to return to normal. Mars employed 1000 people to remove every Bar from every shop in Britain at a cost of three million pounds. The Company immediately withdrew from funding vivisection, bringing their experiments to a halt. The cost to the ALF for this action was about $5 worth of chocolate.

The UK Government responded by setting up a special police branch to focus solely on animal rights activists called ARNI (Animal Rights National Index). This was the first time the animal movement had inflicted a serious dent in a nation's economy, and it scared the bejasus out of them. The ALF admitted it was a hoax a few weeks later.

"The point of it fundamentally was to create a shock wave" explained 'Ben', one of the masterminds behind the operation.

That it certainly did.

Amongst other things, this action underlined the ALF's disinterest in outside opinion, including that of the broader animal rights community. It illustrated how public opinion can be irrelevant when targeting a specific company about a particular issue. This was squarely between the ALF and Mars Co. and the ALF won.

It also demonstrated to those watching the potential impact of this type of action.

The following month, December 1984, bottles of Sunsilk with a large "**X**" scrawled on them began appearing in shops in Dublin, Kilkenny and Limerick.

The Irish ALF alerted the media, claiming they had distributed bottles of Sunsilk laced with bleach in shops across Ireland because the Corporation that produced them – Unilever - engaged in animal experiments. This prompted a major withdrawal of all Sunsilk products from all 14 of Boots stores in Northern Ireland and many in the South.

In the same month animal rights activists contacted the media to claim they have poisoned frozen turkeys on sale in the run up to Christmas. Quinnsworth removed thousands of turkeys from their 35 stores in the Dublin area for inspection. They were all found to be free from rat poison and duly returned to the shelves but still cost the companies concerned dearly while generating plenty of headlines for the activists.

More insidiously in 1990 the ALF contacted media in Cork and threatened to poison water reservoirs in Cork, Kerry and Limerick if the upcoming nationwide Coursing season went ahead. Almost immediately after reporting this in the newspapers, residents in one north Cork Suburb contacted the Council complaining of odd-tasting water. The Council shut off water to 600 homes as they carried out tests. Slightly high counts of chlorine were detected but nothing of concern and the water was tuned back on.

That same year in April, L'Oréal hair products covered in stickers that warned of tampering showed up at numerous shops around Belfast and Lisburn as well as in Britain. The ALF claimed responsibility as L'Oréal removed all hair products from their shelves. This contrasts with the response to the same situation in Britain, where the threat was essentially ignored by the Police and media.

A repeat of the turkey poisoning hoax was attempted in December 1991, this time in Limerick city, when frozen turkey carcasses injected with rat poison turned up in the post at a local newspaper, with notes attached claiming contamination of turkeys nationwide. Whether by accident or design, this action only garnered limited press and it failed to materialize into a full-blown public scare.

Food poisoning hoaxes are an unusual form of direct action because they strongly rely on an outside variable to succeed. A gullible and hysterical mass media are essential, if unwitting, components of this approach. This tactic is guaranteed to generate only negative press for the animal rights activists, though it also typically sheds unwanted light on the targeted company. Despite the fear and panic this tactic can sometimes generate, the fact is no-one ever got ill from consuming products the ALF claimed to have spiked and no-one was ever likely too given these were all hoax's, designed solely to financially damage the targeted companies. This contrasts greatly with the regular and often fatal outbreaks of food poisoning caused by the meat and dairy industry.

In summary, the ALF do not poison people, but animal agriculture does, all the time. Whether its BSE/Mad Cow disease here and in Britian or SARS I and II in Asia, or salmonella, or COVID 19, or listeria, campylobacter, E-Coli, the meat and dairy industry are the actual culprits here. Of the ten thousand or more people who are affected by food poisoning each week in the UK and Ireland, 95% of those are reported to be meat and poultry related.

Despite its clearly anti-social nature, 'food poison hoax's' proved to be remarkably effective when given the oxygen of publicity. The tactic seems to have died out around this time and has not resurfaced.

The ALF in Eire has grown considerably since our small beginnings in early '84, the number of activists has increased and actions are becoming more frequent.

We first came to public attention in Nov. of '84, having claimed bottles of Sunsilk shampoo had been laced with bleach in three counties because of cruel experiments carried out by the company. Front page articles appeared in every national newspaper and police "investigations" started, all to no avail. A national animal rights organisation had its office raided and street campaigners were hassled for information on the activists involved. Actions continued unabaited and a campaign against butcher shops resulted in the Irish Butchers Federation demanding extra protection for their shops.

Currently, we are involved in a highly successful campaign against bloodsports. On 27th August '85, a monument to the worlds most famous hound, situated in Co. Waterford, was tarred by activists who left a note warning "when you fix it up we will f°°° it up". The monument was of Master McGrath, who won the Waterloo Cup three times. This action preceded a number of raids on coursing clubs (in Eire hares are captured and kept for enclosed coursing). On September 26th hares were released from a coursing club in Mitchelstown, Co. Cork and there were other similar raids. In two nights of action, Dec. 10th and Jan. 1st four coursing properties were attacked in Waterford, Kilkenny and Tipperary. Due to the bloodsports fraternitys abhorrence of publicity, they have refused to speak to police or the press after their property has been attacked. The result of which has been little or no police intervention in our activities (as regards anti-coursing action).

Small ALF groups now exist in the South, South-East and East of Eire, with contact between each. There have also been a number of actions carried out by anonymous groups - in March of last year the Canadian Embassy was sprayed with slogans against the seal cull, around the same time 15 butcher shops were attacked, by persons unknown, during a night of action in Cork. Hopefully, the publicity from our recent anti-coursing raids will spark some support from anti-bloodsport factions.

It is marvellous to know ALF activity is growing around the world and we look forward to the day when animal persecution ends, - which it will.

Yours for the liberation of
all animals from suffering,

above - *letter from the Irish ALF to the UK ALF SG Diary of Actions #18, p.33,1986.*

The Belfast ALF persisted with waves of attacks on butchers' shops, fur shops, gun shops and fast-food restaurants throughout the city over the next 5 years. Premises had windows smashed, locks glued, graffiti daubed on walls and fires started. Hunter's vehicles were blown up or set on fire. Crebilly and Dungannon Coursing clubs were yet again visited in 1990 by the ALF. The Dungannon stadium was burned to the ground in an arson attack and was out of action for almost a year, costing the club $250,000.

In response, the RUC established a team of 50 detectives to hunt down those responsible and in 1989 they arrested two men from Belfast – David Cusick and Edward Gilmore – for firebombing a car belonging to a foxhunter.

In 1991, the ALF cell in the North claimed they had received plastic explosives from a sympathetic Provisional IRA member, though the IRA denied this. Whatever the truth, that year saw a spectacular rise in ALF arsons throughout the province. Three pubs that supported hunting were firebombed. Butchers' shops and farmers property was set on fire. The ALF cell bragged in the media about how successful they had been over the last year, claiming 17 separate attacks in the previous 6 months alone.

As if to underline that message, they continued burning shops, fishing boats, hunters' vehicles, and empty buildings of factory farms in a spree that lasted until the end of the 1991. They were so prolific at this time that a prominent Ulster Unionist Party MP urged Brain Mawhinny, the UK Secretary of State and a keen foxhunter himself, to proscribe the ALF under the Emergency Powers Act, meaning membership or even promotion of the group could lead to a prison sentence. This was a useless gesture as the ALF has no membership as such. Nor is there a leadership or any formal structure, it's simply a tactic that expresses itself in action. Whether Mawhinny understood this or not, he refused the request, stating the RUC had adequate resources to deal with them.

He was right.

A 50-strong team of RUC detectives had been following suspects for the previous 3 months before they struck, raiding homes, and arresting 8 people for various ALF offences. One, David Nelson, was held on bail, charged with two counts of planting incendiary devices, one charge of planting a petrol bomb underneath a car, criminal damage and 5 counts of arson. He was already on a suspended sentence when arrested so bail was denied. The RUC brought charges of arson against another 4 people regarding 10 attacks over the previous 18 months.

At their Trial in May 1992 three activists were given prison sentences on charges of arson and criminal damage. David Nelson got 3 and a half years. The other two – Alistair Mullen and Graeme Cambell - got 2 years each on similar charges. Due to his age, Cambell was sent to a Young Offender's institution while the other two were taken to the notorious Maze prison. Cambell appealed his sentence and after 6 months was released. The two judges hearing his case decided his sentence was "too heavy" and immediately suspended it, meaning he was free to go.

"There is no such thing as a friendly chat with a policeman...they will come up to you, put their arm round your shoulder, 'Come on my boy, tell me what happened', don't fall for that trap. If you were cautioned with the words 'you don't have to say anything, but it may harm your defence', just latch onto, 'you don't have to say anything'. Phil Davies, retired Police Chief Superintendent/ current Police Liaison Consultant to the Countryside Alliance (UK) gives advice to fellow hunters at a (leaked) webinar in 2020 organised by the Master of Foxhounds Association on 11th August 2020. The full leaked webinar is available on the HSA website.

CARELESS WHISPERS - Reflecting on his arrest, Cambell admitted naiveté about his rights and the law when faced with well-experienced police interrogators. Despite their 3-month spying operation, the RUC had accrued very little on any of the accused, and nothing of any use. *"The case against us in the end was based solely on admissions made by all eight defendants during police questioning"* he wrote in the ALF (UK) Supporters Group newsletter from Autumn 1992 (p.10). Police alleged they had found his fingerprints on an unexploded incendiary device, and they showed him interview notes from some other defendants that supposedly implicated him in arson attacks on a hunter's car. Faced with this 'evidence', and denied a solicitor, Alistair admitted to some of the charges. *"As I found out later, the other defendants' statements, implicating me, could not be used as evidence against me, and the police didn't have any other evidence on me."*

These three men, all from the same ALF cell, became Ireland first animal rights prisoners and there was a brief hiatus in ALF actions across the North as a result.

Things picked up again in late 1993 when a Belfast McDonalds had its windows smashed and locks glued. In February 1994 the Northern Irish ALF sent a wave of incendiary devices in the post to people involved in blood sports in Britain and Ireland. Some were intercepted but others made it through and caused slight damage when opened.

That summer, a building at Belfast Queens University psychology lab was set on fire and the ALF paid a visit to the Master of the County Down Staghounds but they got the wrong address and attacked the man's fathers house instead. He was himself a retired Master of Staghounds and lived right next door to the intended target.

Later in 1994, a young woman named Nina Wilson was arrested at an animal rights information stall in Belfast city centre. Police accused her of planting a firebomb at Parson and Parson's, a nearby hunter' shop, some two hours earlier.

Nina had moved from her native Cumbria to Belfast a few years earlier to study electronics. She got involved with the local animal rights group and often spent her weekends sabbing foxhunts or running an animal outreach stall in the city.

A few hours before her arrest on that August weekend, Nina had taken some time away from the stall to do a little shopping and had browsed around Parson and Parsons shop looking for a wax jacket to buy. She tried on a few jackets for size and left without making a purchase. Shortly after she left, the ALF phoned the shop to warn the owners of an incendiary device in their store. Police were called and a search was made of the premises. An incendiary device was indeed found, in the pocket of a wax jacket. Police then went directly to the animal rights stall down the street and arrested Nina.

Forensics discovered fibres of Nina's gloves in the pocket of the jacket the incendiary had been left in and paraffin from the device on her gloves. The prosecution thought they had a watertight case. The Crown claimed there was "overwhelming forensics evidence" against Nina and that it would be an "astounding" coincidence if Nina was not the guilty person.

Despite all that, after a 3-day trial Nina was found not guilty. Her defence argued the forensics were botched by Police before the evidence was properly bagged. The Jury agreed. Her supporters in the Courtroom erupted in cheers and Nina was free to carry on her legal campaigning for animals.

FARE PLAY - The **Game and County Fare** in Co. Antrim is a typical showcase for human Dominion and a celebration of all thing's animal abusive. Mr. Brian Titterington is one of the Fares main organizers. Many days in the late 1980's, he must have wished he wasn't. He probably learned to hate the ring of the bell, answering the door to yet another unwanted plumber, concerned paramedic, or smiling pizza delivery guy....

The harassment started off small; slogans painted over adverts for the annual Fayre, held outside Belfast, first appeared in 1984. Such attacks became a yearly feature and soon were combined with direct and regular harassment of the Fayre's organizers. Over the next 5 years, Mr Titterington himself was the subject of over *three hundred* hoax call-outs- every conceivable service was sent to his house including: ambulances, taxis, fire brigade, pizza delivery, more taxis, plumbers, electricians, another ambulance, gardeners, the police, you name it, Brian got it. Repeatedly. His property, including his car, was also regularly vandalized.

It got so bad he was forced to move house in 1989 and went ex-directory, meaning his name, address and phone number no longer appeared in the 'yellow pages' phone book. Believe me this is worse than it sounds, for those of you born after circa 1995. It's a bit like being deplatformed from Facebook. If you were born after 2005, it's like being kicked off TicToc.

Actions culminated in 1994 when animal rights activists (not the ALF) posted 3 letter bombs to organizers of the Fayre, including Mr.Titterington. All 3 devices were intercepted by the police before they got to their targets.

Pressure was even coming from the Free Presbyterian Church, led by bigoted firebrand Ian Paisley. They were mad because the Fayre was happening on a Sunday, the Lords Day of Rest, when even the playgrounds should be closed. Talk about getting shot by both sides.

After the letter bombs, things seem to have quietened down for Mr Titterington and company, as the activists shifted focus to other targets in the area.

The Game and County Fayre continues to this day but went 'virtual' in 2021, in line with Covid restrictions. Which makes it sound even more boring than an actual live Fayre but at least you wouldn't get rained on.

"We will continue to use ruthless methods against ruthless men" anonymous Cork ALF activist.

PROJECTILE REASONING - The prevalence of smashing windows of butcher's shops and fur shops peaked in the late 1980's-early 1990's. The hundreds of attacks listed in the Diary of Actions probably only reflects a portion of what went on - reports in the media at this time tell a story of widespread and underreported acts of vandalism on butchers, field sports shops and furriers across Dublin, Cork, Waterford, and Belfast. Many shops were repeatedly attacked, like Barnardo's furriers in Dublin. Vehicles were often targeted as well. Arrests were made in Belfast, leading ultimately to the imprisonment of three of the cell's members in 1992 but the less-experienced Gardai in the South were unable to "smash the ALF" as they intended. There were a handful of arrests leading to small fines that did nothing to slow down ALF actions.

The tactic slowed down by 2010 – no doubt better security and the prevalence of CCTV inhibited this approach. However, Barnardo's Furriers continue to receive attention from the ALF periodically, along with the owner's home and vehicle.

CHOICE CUTS - One night in Dublin in early April 1987, 20-year old Sean Reily and friend Tim (names changed) met up for a few pints in a local pub. They got talking about animal rights and the recent wave of ALF attacks on city centre shops. Butchers, Furriers, Angling shops, meat delivery vehicles, anything directly involved in the animal trade, were having their windows smashed, locks glued, and slogans spray painted wildly all over their walls. Commuters could not fail to notice the aftermath of these attacks in the mornings following. And not just Dublin. Belfast, Cork, and Waterford had it going on too.

Sean had recently been reading issues of 'Frontline', an ALF periodical, full of action reports and interviews with anonymous activists. Perhaps prompted by this, Sean suggested to his friend they travel that night to a nearby butchers' shop on Tim's motorbike and throw lumps of coal through its windows.

Tim agreed and off they went on Sean's motorbike. When they arrived at McGahans butchers' shop, Tim dismounted and launched one rock of coal at the shop window, but it bounced off. Sean then dismounted and threw his rock straight through the window.

They both immediately got back on the motorbike and sped off, but it wasn't over yet. Splitting up to go their separate ways, Tim went on foot and Sean sped off home on his bike, adrenalin surfing through them both as the sound of crashing glass still ringing in their ears.

Tim was arrested when he arrived at his parent's house. The crash of breaking glass had also rung in the ears of a nearby Garda patrol car and Tim was spotted and silently trailed till he got home. Surprised and caught off-guard, he soon confessed to the act of vandalism and agreed to give evidence in Court.

Police raided Sean's house where he lived with his parents the next day. His father, Sean Sr., a burly retired Garda himself was apoplectic with rage when erstwhile colleagues came to his door waving a search warrant. In Sean's bedroom they found four issues of 'Frontline', an ALF Supporters Group periodical.

Sean continued to deny the charges in Court, even when the prosecution produced the inflammatory magazines, described as 'revolting' by presiding Judge Denis Shields. Sean said he had been given them at an animal rights stall, thought they were 'stupid' but was 'keeping them for a friend'. He denied being in the ALF.

Mitigating evidence, as presented by Sean's father, was that Sean had fallen off a bike and hit his head when aged 12 and had spent six weeks in a coma.

Sean and Tim were both fined $50.

This story was published in the Irish Independent on October 15th 1987.

FANTOM MENACE - On February 11th, 1985, indie legends **The Smiths** released their second album "Meat is Murder".

The following week, February 20th, Cork newspapers described how a 'phantom gang' spray painted this album title on 15 city centre butchers' shops over a single night 'in a well-coordinated action'. Coincidence? Animal activism or extroverted Smiths fans? Maybe both! Who knows! Only the Phantom Gang know! Although the actions were, bizarrely, condemned by the Irish Anti-Vivisection League, Morrisey would have been pleased, if only briefly.

SMASH HITS - In 1987, **CONFLICT** released their *magnum opus* **The Ungovernable Force** album. Songs like the infamous "This is the ALF" explicitly endorsed direct action and guaranteed attention from the UK's Special Branch for years to follow.

Musically, it was a magnificent blend of thrash metal and punk, formulated in large part by the band's guitarist (and ALF activist) at the time, Kevin Webb (RIP). The sonic delivery perfectly complements the urgency and fury of the lyrics, delivered in a near-hysterical primal scream. Clocking in at about a half hour of music in total, this album is an almost perfect emotional time-capsule of articulated punk rage in Thatcher's Britain. Flyers with maps on them pinpointing butchers' shops in the area and encouraging attack were sometimes passed around at their gigs (by fans, not the band).

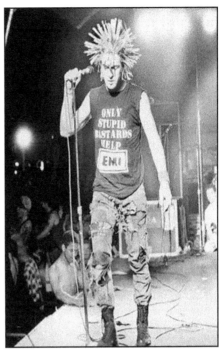

above left - **CONFLICT's** Kevin Webb (RIP), ALF activist and punk rock guitarist extraordinaire – perfected a magnificent blend of punk and thrash metal on Conflicts magnum opus **The Ungovernable Force** (1986). When they entered the studio – Rockfield in Wales- they had nothing written or planned and requested they be left alone for a few days while they figured out what to do. What emerged was a driving, rapid-firing cacophony that, at times, just manages to maintain itself but never disappears into noise. Soaring melodies weave in and out of the pulsating rhythms, all threaded together by splices of news reports and film dialogue (the nuclear-war movie Threads is heavily sampled). Source Conflict archive.

The United States has a similar vegan/punk movement called Hardcore, but it had a (in my view) disappointingly flattened, repetitive sound that further limited the genres appeal. Nevertheless, bands like Earth Crisis fostered a frenzied, passionate following, with much of that energy directed into militant groups like the Animal Liberation Front and the newly-emerging Earth Liberation Front.

Straight Edge anti-drug philosophy was also closely tied to the US phenomenon.

above right - CONFLICT's Colin Jerwood. Conflict explicitly endorsed direct action in their music and imagery. Songs like "This is the A.L.F." guaranteed them attention from Special Branch and the Animal Rights National Index, the UK Police database on animal activists, for years to follow.

An article about the ALF in Dublin's Evening Herald from September 8th, 1986 (p.17) contained an interesting roundup of the numerous small scale but persistent actions being carried out by individuals and small groups all around the Republic in the name of animal rights. Their estimation of 100 active ALF members in the Republic is a Gardai figure so it's hard to know how accurate it is, particularly as the Police had very little success in apprehending anyone and were clearly confused by the phenomenon. It's reasonable to assume the Garda Siochana - institutionally and individually - had absolutely no reference points for this type of illegal activity. They simply didn't know where to begin. Rarely having met a vegetarian, never mind a vegan militant activist, they simply couldn't get into the heads of people who would do this kind of thing. That's why they arrested and held for questioning Pat Phelan, the elderly head of ICABS during the 1980's and 90's, twice. Despite his frequent public condemnation of all things ALF, and his old age, the Gardai didn't know where else to turn. The lack of many formal animal welfare/rights groups in Ireland at the time didn't help them either - there was precious little to spy on or infiltrate, unlike the UK.

The last paragraph of the article reads " *ALF people in England have served prison sentences of two years*". Within a few years of this being published, ALF activists were getting sent down for up to 10 years (Ronnie Lee) and by the mid 1990's, activists were being sentenced to up to 14- and 18-year stretches (Keith Mann and Barry Horne respectively).

If the Gardai were right in their estimation, then those 100 (at most) ALF activists punched well above their weight. Their actions forced the issue of animal cruelty and rights into the public spotlight where it's been ever since. Societies cosy consensus on animal exploitation had to be challenged and combatted if the issue was ever to be taken seriously. Silent vigils and the odd letter in the local newspaper just wasn't going to cut it.

The Animal Liberation Front - helping animals out since 1976.

"If we are vandals then so are those who destroyed forever the gas chambers of Buchenwald and Auschwitz"- anonymous ALF activist.

above - ***Paranoid Visions' Deko Dachau*** *leads the shout-a-long in Dublin, circa early 1990's. Paranoid Visions, along with Belfast's* **F.U.A.L.** *were early and vocal supporters of the ALF. Source Paranoid Visions archive.*

"For the first few months of 1977, the Roxy – a black hole in the wet London streets-drained all the painted sewer rats and played host to a phenomenon. Out from the dark caves, where anarchy had hidden his face these last years, out again in the streets, the voice of hope, the cry of a future that was buried in the narcotic fuck-up of the sixties. Punk came out to air his dirty wings, crashing out from the stagnant mire that was the Beach Boys sperm in Malibu Beach, the Beatles death-picking in Madison Square Garden – the Pistols, The Dammed, The Clash – new sounds, new vocabulary. The dirty little Roxy bounced to the new energy, and Wall Street and the City pricked up their dollar ringing ears.

Within six months the new anarchy was bought out, the capitalist counterrevolutionaries killed with cash. Punk went from being a movement of change to become the biggest media burn-out since 'Hippy'. In six months, it became a burnt-out memory of how it might have been.

Bought up, cleaned up, souped up. Just another cheap product for the consumer-head." Crass, opening monologue on side 3 of Christ the Album.

In short, Punk was *way* too vital and energising to be solely left to the poseurs, hypocrites and drug addicts that made up much of the first wave of the movement. Anar*chy* in the UK? No! Anarch*ists* in the UK!

Outrage at the bloated, self-indulgent pomposity of Stadium Rock – first wave punks' nemesis - was turned outward. 'The System' was the new enemy, not overlong guitar solos by men dressed like Gandalf.

This fresh emphasis was the galvanising factor behind Punk Part Two.

Music composer Jim Steinman, the man who wrote bombastic hits like 'Bat Out of Hell' amongst many others, described his music in six words – 'Feverish, Strong, Romantic, Violent, Rebellious, Fun.'

These same nouns perfectly sum up the essence of Punks second wave - anarcho punk. To be clear, despite its often militaristic and confronting aesthetic, anarcho punk was not itself a violent movement. Its progenitors – Crass- were explicitly pacifist and frequently denounced violence, revolutionary or otherwise, in their lyrics and other media. But it did attract violence. Police, skinheads and others frequently targeted punks and punk gigs. The media, including the music press, usually either blatantly ignored or cynically caricatured the movement.

*"And **Crass**: their power lies in their ecstatic clinging to the ideas that bred them, and which they continue to propagate with burning venom. Those who criticise them for being one-dimensional miss out on that most important point: that **therein** lies their greatness."* David Tibet reviews a Crass gig in Nottingham, *circa* early 1980's

Time and Pressure creates diamonds, however, and being locked out of the dominant cultural narrative meant the anarcho punks had to create their own. Squats, communes, fanzines, shared living, music, food and politics all combined to form an underground culture that dovetailed neatly with the emerging animal rights scene. Anarcho-punk and grassroots animal activism were made for each other, a perfect match. Grass Roots Direct Action is the lifeblood of both indeed, the OG of the ALF, Ronnie Lee, was himself a punk, singing in a band called Total Attack. They even recorded a demo tape and got a friend who worked at BBC Radio to leave it unannounced on John Peels desk one day. They hoped he would listen to the music then play it on his radio show but because the parcel had anonymously appeared on his desk rather than through the usual route, Peel grew suspicious and threw it into a bin filled with water, thus ending the bands commercial ambitions. Now *that's* punk rock.Punks' loss was the Animals' gain as now Ronnie and fellow ex-bandmates (all activists themselves) could devote themselves full time to militant animal rights activism.

COMBAT ROCK – above - ***Ronnie Lee***, *co-founder of the ALF, singing in the short-lived **Total Attack**. Here they are live in Slough no less, 1980. Stock image.*

NOTHING SUCCEEDS LIKE SUCCESS – Animal activism provided arenas where success was achievable and tangible. Hunts can be sabotaged by a small group with few resources. As with economic sabotage and animal liberation. Small battles in a big war perhaps, but this is how victory is won.

Unlike the drudgery and impotence of many of the big CND-type rallies at the time, the pursuit of animal rights was immediate and rewarding to its participants. This wasn't submissive protest, pleading for change with those in power; it was self-directed resistance where small numbers of people could have an outsized impact in a 'target-rich' enviornment. The stark, black and white aesthetic of the anarcho punk scene chimed with the bleak, often violent, imagery and reportage from the animal rights movement.

A million people in a factory and office/Aware there's something missing/living with the losses/War in your bedroom/bodies in your fridge/Domestic violence/ the tomb you dig. Crass, Heard too much about,1979.

THE IMPORTANCE OF BEING EARNEST – above - *The mighty **CRASS** at full throttle. Described live as a band "forever on the verge of exploding", Crass set the stage for the anarcho-punk movement in the early 1980's. Their vision of anarchism included animal rights and pacifism as well as feminism and atheism. Crass were the bridge between the declining Hippy movement and upcoming Punk, combining members from both camps. The 16th Century farmhouse they operated from was listed as a Grade 2 property in 2001, when Penny Rimbaud, Crass's drummer and co-founder, managed to persuade the Council of the cultural and political significance of the building. Since occupying the house in 1967, Rimbaud and others launched the Stonehenge free festival, Crass, the anarcho punk movement and many other projects. Stock image.*

A Relic haunts the Left – the Relic of Speciesism! Of course, not all animal rights activists were or are anarchists or punks, but most tend to be on the left of the spectrum. The funny thing about that spectrum is the further Left one goes the more hostile to animal rights one gets. Critics like to accuse the hard left of seeing oppression everywhere. This is clearly not the case when it comes to animals, quite the contrary. Marx and Marxists have typically displayed the same brutal contempt toward non-human animals as the old Manchester Mill factory owners of the 19th century showed their proletarian workforce. Engels was openly mocking of the Fabian Socialists vegetarianism, popular amongst middle class bohemians at the time. Then and now, concern for animal well-being is often seen as, at very best, a distraction and at worse a betrayal of the class struggle, the only struggle that matters. Bourgeois sentimentality has no place in the revolution and what will the proletariat eat if they can't eat cows?

All this is a shame because much of what Marx wrote about is easily transferable to the area of animal-human relations. The pinnacle of human nature, and the whole point of the ideal Society is, according to Marx, *Species-Being* -the fulfilment of the individual's life potential, the freedom to move unhindered and engage in tasks and relationships that bring meaning and happiness to our lives. He was referring only to humans of course but one can apply the same principle to any other sentient animal. In which case, the most oppressed creature in a factory farm is not the worker on small wages, it's the chickens in small cages.

Thankfully there now exists a vocal minority of Marxists who interweave vegan philosophy with Marxism, including American academic Corey Lee Wrenn who has written extensively on animals and speciesism in Ireland.

"Germany got the Bader-Meinhof gang, Britain got Punk" Penny Rimbaud, Crass.

AND WE WILL CELEBRATE WITH SUCH FIERCE DANCING THE DEATH OF YOUR INSTITUTIONS

Punks at the (ex-Police) 'Station' anarchist venue in Gateshead, North East England, circa 1986, But it could have been any of the many similar venues in the UK and Ireland at the time. Note the intimacy and physicality of those in the photo here. Venues like this one, and Warzone in Belfast, were dotted around the UK and provided space for the anarcho punk movement to flourish. ALF and Hunt Sab numbers were boosted by the involvement of such punks from the early 1980's on. Their rebellious energy and sense of urgency influenced the tone and attitude of the animal rights movement. Despite its aggressive posturing and symbology, Anarcho-punk was not an inherently aggressive scene but it did often attract violence from opposing social forces - Police, fascists and royalists in particular. The exuberance and passion of its cohorts was often mistaken for menace by outside Society, but the reality was a very warm, positive and capable movement. A network of like-minded people built an underground society that ran parallel to the mainstream and sought to reshape that mainstream via mutual aid and direct action. Photo by Chris Killip.

KILLER WAILS -above - **CRASS live** – *a band "**forever on the verge of exploding**". Crass were the Ground Zero of the second wave of punk, rejecting the individualistic nihilism so prevalent in Punks' prime movers. They offered a phenomenal take on the world that places them outside the confines of Punk, Rock or even Music. The space they occupied was much bigger than that. At their best, Crass produced a sound unlike any other before or since. Lyrically poetic and sonically abrasive, they proposed a way of life utterly diametric to the common consensus. Living together in an old farmhouse in rural Essex, Crass established a record label and distribution network to record and promote themselves and the many other bands that were inspired by them. Stock image.*

WE WILL USE RUTHLESS METHODS

against ruthless men

A chronology of direct actions by the Animal Liberation Front and adjacent groups

All information in this chapter has been obtained through one or more of the following sources – the Irish Newspaper Archive, ALF Supporters Group Newsletters and Diary of Action publications, HOWL magazine, Bite Back magazine, Unoffensive Animal website and the Talon Conspiracy website. Archives of newspapers not included in the Irish Newspaper Archive, including the Galway Advertiser, included also.

1964

January, Northern Ireland, Co Antrim - persons unknown cut a large hole in cages holding hares due to be Coursed, forcing cancellation of the upcoming meet at Crebilly Coursing Club. Police speculate it was either the work of pranksters or "those opposed to blood sports". Crebilly Coursing Club will make many an appearance in this Timeline. (1)

1982

January, Waterford - three masked men, one armed with a shotgun, raid Whitford Polo Grounds Coursing club, holding a security guard at gunpoint, and release 40 hares from cages. (1)

May, County Mayo, Inishkea Islands - Dublin **Sea-Shepherd** volunteers are joined by fellow Shepherds and Hunt Sabs from the UK in an 8-week mission on the tiny Inishkea Islands off the coast of Mayo in the West of Ireland. The Irish State was planning to kill the local grey seal population because fishermen complained they were 'stealing' 'their' fish. Fishermen had slaughtered over 100 seal pups the year before by shooting them in the face. They threatened to do the same again unless the Government carried out a cull. The State made two attempts to begin the cull but backed down in the face of determined opposition from the Sea Shepherd crew. The ten Shepherds, living in tents and an old, abandoned Police station, stayed on at the Islands for about two weeks until all the seal pups had matured and taken to the open sea, safe from the bullets of fishermen. (2)

Sea Shepherd returned to the islands again in 1983 but the Government announced there would be no more culls. Seals are a protected species in Irish law.

October, Belfast - fur shop in city attacked twice over the month by the **ALF.** (3)

November, Belfast – the same fur shop and 1 mink farm daubed with paint and ALF symbol. (4)

December, Dublin, and Meath - Hunt Saboteurs disrupt the Fingal Harriers and the Meath Foxhounds with antimate spray and horn calls in Irelands first known acts of hunt sabotage since Fr. Eugene Sheehy and the local GAA sabbed the Limerick Bruree Foxhounds out of existence in 1886. (5)

Co. Tyrone, Crebilly Coursing Club - Direct Activists from the Queens University Belfast Anti-Bloodsports Society - described as 'Communists' by the Coursers - blockade and invade the Crebilly stadium during its annual Coursing Festival - violence and arrests ensue amid lots of media interest. The ALF had cut holes in the cages keeping the Hares the night before and 50 hares had escaped. (6)

1983

January, Co. Dublin - Hunt Saboteurs from Dublin are joined by comrades from across the UK and sabotage an impressive 4 hunts in 4 days of intense activity. Twenty

Saboteurs successfully hit the Tara Harriers, West Meath Foxhounds, Louth Foxhounds and Goldburn Beagles despite violence and threats from enraged hunters and their support. The West Meath hunt were the most aggressive, with 7 sabs getting attacked by a mob of 40 hunt support. (1)

Eglish, Co. Tyrone - 50 activists from the Queens University Belfast Anti-Bloodsports Society once again stage a sit-down blockade at a Hare Coursing meet, causing significant disruption, and gaining lots of media attention. This confrontational tactic was new to the island and stood in contrast to the 'silent vigils' held by the moribund Anti Live Hare Coursing Society. (2)

New blood was entering the debate with a fresh urgency and tactics.

March, Dublin - Seven Sea Shepherds stage a sit-down protest inside the Canadian Embassy, protesting the Country's annual seal cull. (3)

August, Co. Down - 8 hens liberated from a battery "farm" near Castlereagh. Damage also inflicted on premises. (3)

November - UK Sea Shepherds, fresh from keeping an eye on grey seals off the coast of Mayo, join forces with Belfast Hunt Sabs and hit 3 separate hunts over a week. This was part of a skill-sharing weekend gathering between activists from both Islands. Meanwhile Dublin activists were busy sabbing Beagle hunts in their area. (5)

1984

February, N. Ireland - fox-traps destroyed near Omagh. (1)

ONE HIT WONDER - June, Dublin - Animal activists going under the name the **Green Moles** raid premises of the Eastern Health Board and rescue several guinea pigs and rabbits. Anti-vivisection slogans sprayed on walls of lab. Activists described filthy conditions the animals were being kept in to the media after the raid (2). The Green Moles do not appear again in the historical record.

Belfast - Adverts for the upcoming Game and Country fair damaged and covered in slogans. (3)

July, Waterford - 3 vehicles at a poultry farm in Cappaquin have paint stripper thrown over them by ALF; 3 butchers shops damaged with graffiti and paint bombs; advert hoardings for dead turkey's spray painted. (4)

August, Waterford - two unnamed local activists arrested and prosecuted for damaging butchers' shops. These two unknown individuals become the Republic of Irelands first animal activists to be prosecuted by the State. They were fined $30 each and ordered to pay Court costs.

Later that month 7 butchers' shops in the city have locks glued, paint thrown over them and/or windows smashed. (5)

September, Dublin – an angling shop in city has locks glued up and paint thrown over premises. (6)

October, Co. Cork - PRETTY VACANT - ALF release 85 hares being held in cages by local Coursing club in Ballyellis. (7)

November, Co. Armagh- Scuffles break out at Crebilly Coursing Clubs' Ulster Cup when animal activists blockade the Clubs entrance. 25 activists from the **Belfast Animal Rights Movement** hold a sit-down at the entrance of the Venue and ignore police requests to move so had to be dragged away forcibly. (8)

December, Dublin, Limerick, and Kilkenny - stocks of Sunsilk shampoo removed from shop shelves following a claim made to the media and police by the ALF claiming some products had been contaminated with bleach. Sunsilk, owned by Unilever, experiment on animals. (9)

December, Dublin - Animal activists claim, via, phone calls to the media, they have poisoned turkeys on sale in shops in the run-up to Christmas. Police report they are taking this threat seriously. Thousands of turkeys from 35 Quinnsworth stores are removed and inspected by experts who conclude the threat to be a hoax. Turkeys then returned to stores. (10)

December, Co. Antrim - scuffles with police break out when a 100-strong crowd of anti-blood sports activists from the **Anti-Bloodsports Society** try to push through the police and blockade the entrance to the Crebilly Coursing event (again). No injuries but two arrests made. (11)

Dungannon, N. Ireland - ALF hit same Coursing club twice in two nights- the first night they set free 40 hares; the next night they return to tear down half the fencing around the Coursing field. (12)

Galbally, Co. Limerick - 15 activists from the **Wildlife Protection Group** break into a Coursing compound and release all of the 90 hares being kept there. The activists then set about destroying the compound before scattering broken glass around the coursing field. In a phone call to the media the Group promise further action. (13)

1985

January, Dublin - 3 animal abuse businesses attacked in the Sandymount area of Dublin on the same night- windows smashed and slogans painted. (1)

February, Cork - 15 different butchers' shops have "Meat is Murder' painted in large red letters on their walls and windows by a **'phantom gang'** of animal rights activists in a 'well-coordinated' night of action. Action condemned by the Anti-vivisection Society. (2)

March, Dublin- Vivisection lab at UCD is hit twice in one month - slogans daubed on walls and damage done to facility. Slogans against seal cull daubed on Canadian embassy. (3)

Waterford - slogans daubed on house of local hare courser. (4)

April, Dublin - multiple butchers shop windows smashed by ALF. (5)

May, Waterford - 7 snares taken from woodland. (6)

Dublin - fur shop window smashed. (7)

August, Waterford - the famous 'Master McGrath' monument is vandalised with tar and feathers poured over it. The local Coursing Club commisioned the monument to commemorate a particularly successful greyhound from 100 years ago. Note left at monument threatening more action if it is repaired. (8)

September, Mitchelstown, Co. Cork - ALF sabotage local Coursing field by spreading tacks and broken glass on the land. Captive hares also set free. (9)

November, Bandon, Co. Cork - ALF once again target local Coursing Club, spreading 100lbs of glass and 10lb of tacks on the field. Club forced to move location. (10)

December, Co. Cork - Bandon, Cashel and Whitfield Coursing Clubs are all attacked by the ALF with glass and tacks once again spread on land designated for Coursing events. Hundreds of hares released back into the wild and damage done to Coursers' farms. (11)

Dublin - 3 butchers' shops have windows smashed: 4 trucks at an abattoir damaged. (12)

"Slash tyres, glue up locks, butchers, burger bars, the furriers, smash windows, bankrupt the lot, throw paint over shops and houses, paint stripper works great on cars, chewing gum sticks well to fur coats, a seized engine just won't start" Conflict, 'This is the ALF.'

1986

January, Waterford - butchers shop damaged; home of local courser attacked. (1)

Dublin - 3 butchers and a fur shop in city centre have windows smashed. (2)

Kilkenny - ALF spread glass and tacks on Coursing fields in Ballyragget. An 'army'* of Coursing supporters arrived soon after the discovery of tacks to clear the field, delaying the event by only 50 minutes. (3)

John Fitzgerald from ICABS writes to the Mayo News to point out there's been a "massive increase" in attacks on Courser's property by the ALF over the last two months. "A Coursing Club can arrange for a venue to be guarded for up to three weeks prior to an event. But what happens after that? It could be attacked at any time...consider carefully before a valuable field becomes a target for the militants" he suggested.

An "Army" that consisted of people whose prime skill was in setting two dogs on one terrified hare probably wouldn't last long in actual combat.

February, Co. Cork - Violence flares at the annual National Coursing Cup in Clonmel when, allegedly, ALF activists join some militant ICABS members in forming a human blockade across 2 of the 3 entrances to the car park of the stadium where the event was taking place. Blood sports enthusiasts and Police subsequently attack the demonstrators. (4)

"They're a shower of madmen...shotguns will be pulled"- coursing enthusiast and farmer John Drennan threatens his local ALF.

May, Kilkenny - A Farmer who allowed his land to be used by the local Coursing Club has glass and tacks spread on his property. The man went to Court to seek damages for this action but lost when it was discovered the sabotaged land was back in use within a few days - (after exhaustive combing of the field); A nearby Coursing field in Ballyragget is also sabotaged. (5)

June, - ALF repeat threats of more sabotage to anyone involved in Coursing via letters to the local media throughout the Country. Police state they are taking these threats seriously. (6)

September, Dublin newspaper the Evening Herald report extensively on the growing number of ALF attacks around the country recently including - hundreds of hares released from a west Cork Coursing club; a Dublin fur shop and butchers' shop were stink bombed and vandalized, two furriers in Dublin city had their locks superglued for the 4th time in a month, plus KFC and multiple butchers' shops have had their windows smashed. Police estimate there are about 100 ALF activists in Ireland but only two people have been successfully prosecuted so far. Anarcho-punks wearing ALF insignia in Dublin city centre are periodically arrested and questioned but no charges are ever brought. (7)

September, Co. Kilkenny - ALF spread glass and tacks on the land of a pro-coursing farmer. Glass also spread on nearby Seven Horses 7-acre coursing field. Farmer J. Drennan described the attackers as a **"shower of madmen"** and warned **"shotguns will be pulled"** if they attempt doing this again. Police later raid a home in Kilkenny town and claim they've confiscated ALF propaganda. (8)

October, Co. Limerick -ALF sabotage coursing fields in Glin with glass and tacks. (9)

October, Co. Cork - A mob of blood sports fanatics attack a group of **ICABS** (Irish Council Against Blood Sports) members who were attending a coursing meet incognito. One of them was a locally elected **Fine Gael** councillor. They were there to discreetly bear witness but not protest the event and the crowd were unaware of their affiliations until police approached them and identified the five as ICABS activists. The Coursing crowd then turned on them, accusing the 5 of being ALF activists. Police had to quickly escort them away from the grounds under a barrage of insults, kicks, and punches. (10)

November, Co. Kerry- Listowell Coursing Club forced to relocate their annual meet to a secret out-of-town address after receiving threats of sabotage from the ALF. (11)

December, Co. Kerry - ALF spread glass and tacks on Ballybeggan Coursing Club racecourse. Tacks are painted grass-green to make them extra hard to discover. (12)

Belfast - 3 butchers' shops have their windows smashed; a school's animal house was raided, and 7 rats liberated; Organiser of the Game and Country Fair has his car repainted and a fur shop in the city was spray painted. (13)

"The grassroots lunatic fringe appear to have succeeded" Dublin's Southern Star on the ALF's war on the fur trade, Jan 31,1987.

January, Co. Limerick - ALF spread broken glass and tacks on land of Clounanna Coursing Club. The Club mount a round-the-clock vigil to prevent future attacks. (1)

January, Dublin - ALF phone police and claim to have planted two incendiary devices in Switzers fur store in the city centre. Store and surrounding streets evacuated for an hour. The Bomb Squad are sent in to search for any suspect devices. (2)

"The Animal Liberation Front has *a point to make"*- Irish Press editorial, Jan24, 1987

Pat Phelan, ICABS chairperson and regular denouncer of the ALF, is arrested and held overnight for questioning in relation to the recent attacks on Coursing Clubs around the county.

ICABS appoint regional 'managers' to keep a lookout for any potential sympathy for the ALF amongst its membership. Mr. Phelan admits many ICABS members secretly admire the ALF. Pat is released without charge the next day. (3)

Irish Coursing Club refer in media to a recent ICABS protest where one 'activist' was wearing a fur coat at the demo! When jeered at by the Coursers for such hypocrisy, said woman took the coat off, turned it inside out and put it back on. To more jeers from the Coursing crowd, presumably. Unfortunately, no photographs exist of this incident.

Dublin- ALF pour petrol through the letterbox at the offices of the Irish Meat Exporters Company. They then set fire to the petrol. Walls of building spray painted with slogans. Minimum damage caused. (4)

Dublin - Incendiary device destined for a fur farm in Co. Laois is intercepted at the General Post Office when the ALF phone the GPO warning of the package - the activists were concerned it might go off at the GPO prematurely. Bomb squad called in; city centre closed for 2 hours. Device erupts into flames when the bomb squad try to diffuse it. (5)

Co. Limerick, Cloununna Coursing Club once again visited by the ALF and has tacks spread on 8 of its fields. The Irish Coursing Cup is due to take place here soon. Security beefed up, at enormous financial cost to the Club. (6)

Co. Cork - Pat Phelan and ICABS treasurer Nuala McNamara arrested again under section 30 of the Offences Against the State Act. Both are held overnight for more questions about the recent ALF activity in Cork. Both released without charge. Both use the media attention to unhesitatingly condemn the ALF for their "outrageous" behaviour of late. (7)

Dublin city centre - ALF phone in bomb threats at multiple locations around the city. One suspect device found but army bomb disposal robot unable to remove device, which turns out to be a telephone book in Christmas paper wrapping. Police admit having trouble apprehending the activists- "the ALF are a very mysterious group" they state. (8)

Dublin city centre- USIT travel agency has windows smashed because they were promoting bullfighting trips to Spain. (9)

Belfast- 9 shops - mostly butchers - have locks glued and windows smashed. (10)

February, Dublin- ALF set fire to 2,000 bales of hay at a farm in Swords. The family who owns the farm were in the newspapers recently for shooting 3 Alsatian pups who were on their land. (11)

Co. Cork -ALF spread tacks on land that had recently been used by a local Coursing club in Clonakilty. (12)

March, Dublin - ALF burn down a storehouse belonging to the Department of Agricultures' Pig-Testing station. Fire Brigade manage to contain fire to this one building (13); Also in Dublin city a fishmongers van was paint stripped twice and a medical animal research laboratory in Beaumont was trashed causing $35,000 in damages. Medical research rooms were destroyed as were some vehicles. (14)

Co. Cork, Clonmel - ICABS join forces with the **Catholic Association for Defence of Animals** and hold a protest outside Clonmel Garda Station. The two groups claim that the police are unfairly accusing them of ALF activities, stating the police are in cahoots with the local Coursing club and are abusing their powers to harass legal campaigners because they have no other leads. Gardai dismiss these allegations. 'Absolute rubbish' they lie. (15)

May, Dublin - Hyland's butcher shop petrol bombed with two devices. This is the shops third visit from the ALF recently. The Butcher suggested the shop is targeted because of the many alleyways in the area, making it easy to escape. That, and the fact they have tortured animal carcass on display in their window. (16)

"But it does prove what one or two misguided people can achieve"- Maureen Fox on the recent spate of ALF attacks, Cork Examiner, Jan12,1987.

June, Dublin - The Pat Kenny radio show interview two balaclava'd members of the ALF about the recent wave of attacks in Dublin city. The Activists claim they are in touch with ALF UK and are in possession of incendiary devices as used to devastating effect in shops all over the UK. The Minister for Communications orders a report into why RTE were giving airtime to the likes of the ALF. (17); Butchers shop window smashed in Glasnevin. (18)

July - ALF claim to have contaminated random bottles of Wella shampoo in stores around the country. Wella has connections with commercial-use vivisection. Product removed and restocked with new product. (19)

Belfast - Pork delivery van covered in glue and paint; KFC in city has its windows smashed. (20)

August, Belfast - Butchers shop, a fast-food restaurant and a meat delivery van all have windows smashed. (21)

October, Co. Cork - ALF set fire to 300 bales of hay and an outbuilding at a farm believed to be involved in hare coursing. Wrong farm was chosen, their intended target was the adjacent farm. (22)

Dublin - 20-year-old Sean O'Neil is fined $50 for throwing a lump of coal through a local butcher's window last April. O'Neil had travelled on a motorbike with an accomplice to McGavans butchers in Phibsboro and threw two lumps of coal at the window. One bounced off. Police apprehended both and when they searched Sean' bedroom they found 4 copies of the ALF magazine 'Frontline' - described as a 'revolting magazine' by the presiding Judge. Seans light fine for the offence may be because his father was a retired cop. Seans' accomplice also convicted but media don't mention his punishment - presumably also a fine. (23)

Co. Cork - Happy to ignore the attack on ICABS members at a Coursing meet last October, Middleton Coursing Club issue an open invite to all members of the ALF to attend a local coursing meet to see how harmless the 'sport' really is. They seem to forget the ALF regularly visit Coursing Clubs, but only at nightime. (24)

Belfast - ALF start a fire at Associated Egg Packers Co. on the outskirts of the city. Police manage to control blaze. (25)

November, Co. Westmeath - Farmer Brendan Farley, Secretary of local Coursing Club, receives a letter from the ALF threatening arson and violence against him and his property if he continues his involvement with the Club.

John Fitzgerald of the **Campaign Against Blood sports** is accused of sending this and many similar letters received by pro-Coursing farmers across the region. Police arrest and prosecute John but the trial collapses due to a technicality. Re-trail is scheduled. (26)

October - Dungannon, N. Ireland - activists spread 'fake news' in the media that Dungannons upcoming Coursing meet has been cancelled due to a disease outbreak amongst the captive hares. (27)

1988

January, Co. Cork, - J. Fitzgerald's trial resumes - John accused of sending out many threatening letters to other pro-Coursing farmers, like the one received by Mr. Farley last November. The letters are all handwritten and begin with '**Dear Scum'.**

John claims he was threatened with having glass shoved down his throat if he didn't confess to the letters at the Garda station and signed a confession of guilt. John later withdrew the confession in Court, claiming it was signed under duress. Jury fails to reach a verdict. Trial collapses for second time. (1)

"How would you like it if I shoved this piece of glass down your throat?" – Detective M. Canlon plays Bad Cop while interviewing ALF suspect J. Fitzgerald.

Later in January the State announce they are dropping all charges against John. (2)
April, Dublin - ALF claim responsibility for a spate of attacks on butchers' shops around the city centre- three butchers' shops in Lennox Street and Sutton Street have windows smashed and paint bombs thrown over them. (3)

June, Co. Cork – More Pro-Coursing farmers in the region receive letters from anonymous animal activists threatening sabotage of their land if they persist in their 'sport'. Macroom Councillor Nora Murphy condemns the threats in the local media. Unusually, the letters also threaten physical violence to any farmers who get in the activists' way. (4)

September, Co. Limerick - ALF contact local media to state they have once again spread tacks on the lands of the Estate of the Earl of Glin due to his continued involvement in coursing. Gardai are investigating. (5)
October, Co. Wexford - newly-cleaned "**Master McGrath**" statue of a prize-winning Coursing greyhound from last century is unveiled at Ballymacmagee after twice being redecorated by the ALF - paint, and then tar and feathers, were thrown over the statue in recent attacks. $2000 was spent on cleaning the statue up. (6)

March, Ulster, Mr Albert Titterington, organiser of Ulster's Games and Country Fair claims a campaign of hate and harassment has been waged against him and his property by the ALF. Over 300 separate incidents have been recorded, ranging from hoax callouts to the fire brigade, ambulance service, taxis, pizza delivery, you name it, 'he' ordered it- to vandalism of his property. The constant attention forced Mr Titterington to move house and go ex-directory from the phone book. (1)

Belfast - Two Belfast men - **David Cusick** and **Edward Gilmore** - arrested and accused of firebombing a car belonging to a foxhunter. Both held in custody. (2)

May, Dublin - A McDonalds in Dun Laoighaire is closed when the ALF phone in a bomb scare to a local Garda station. Police believe it to be a hoax but shut store down for a search anyway. Police also search other branches of McDonalds in the area. (3)

August, Dublin - ALF send threatening letters to two officials from the Dept. Of Agriculture demanding the Department stop leasing land to Coursing clubs. (4)

Pat Phelan of ICABS and the Green Party condemn the threats. (5)

Despite Pats age, his regular condemnation of the ALF and the fact the police have twice brought him in for questioning recently and found zero evidence on him, 'Independent' newspaper columnist John Martin writes that Pat is still not doing enough to distance himself and his organization from 'the militants'. (6)

September, Co. Waterford - Sir Hugh Downey of the Whitfield Estate in Waterford stops allowing the local Coursing club using his land after receiving threatening letters from the ALF. Club forced to find new venue. (7)

"The ALF are a very mysterious group"- Gardai announce a new unit set up to investigate and 'smash' the ALF. SPOLIER ALERT – the Gardai do not smash the ALF. The ALF do, however, continue to smash things.

Five other farmers receive similar threats. John Fitzgerald of the Campaign Against Blood sports once again arrested on suspicion of sending these letters. Police claim in Court that they found 32 similar letters waiting to be posted in Fitzgerald's' house when they raided it. Mr Fitzgerald claims that the police themselves wrote these letters and threw them out the accused bedroom window, then blamed him for writing and then attempting to dispose of the evidence. Mr Fitzgerald is cleared of all charges. Police fabricate denying fabricating evidence. (8)

Enniscorthy, Co. Wexford - Activists release hares from Coursing Club enclosure twice in one week but the hares are rounded up on both occasions. The Clubs walls are daubed with slogans including "A.L.F." Despite all this, the Club state they believe the work was done by vandals, not anti -blood sports activists. The Club mount a 24-hr guard to prevent future acts of vandalism. (9)

December, Belfast - ALF claim to have 'spiked' L'Oréal products with paint stripper in retaliation for the companies continued use of animals in commercial research. Tampered Products with ALF warning stickers placed on them turn up in shops in Lisburn and Belfast. Threat spreads south of the border and leading stores in cities in the Republic withdraw L'Oréal products from their shelves in a major operation (10); Also in Belfast, ALF attack a fur shop and a leather shop in the city centre - paint thrown over properties and "blood dealers' written on walls. (11)

1990

The prestigious Iveagh Harriers foxhunt go out in all their 'splendour' on Boxing Day – a big day in the hunter's calendar – and their dogs 'riot'. The pack descend on an old lady's garden. The frenzied pack rip apart her beloved pet Highland Terrier and the local media turn on the Hunt. Public outrage at their behaviour prompts local hunt saboteurs to focus solely on the Iveagh Harriers for the rest of the season. Saboteurs are so effective that the Harriers cancel all upcoming weekend meets for the rest of the season. (1)

April, Belfast - ALF spike L'Oréal hair products again - 8 tampered devices show up at stores across Ulster with notes of warning attached to them. Stock withdrawn and shops on high alert across the Country. (2)

"This product has been contaminated by the ALF – do not use" -ALF warning sticker attached to a 'poisoned' bottle of shampoo, Belfast 1990.

May, N. Ireland - ALF burn down a hut used by Crebilly Coursing Club. (3)

July, Belfast - ALF damage vehicle and billboards belonging to the Ballymena Game and Country Fair organisation. (4)
September, Co. Tyrone - Oaks Park Stadium in Dungannon set on fire by ALF, causing $250,000 in damages. Stadium out of action for a year. (5)

ALF repeat warnings via media to greyhound tracks all over the country to stay away from Coursing events or face sabotage. (6)

Munster - ALF threaten to poison water supplies to Cork, Kerry and Limerick counties if the upcoming Coursing season goes ahead. Cork County Council and Gardai state they are taking threat 'very seriously'. (7)

October, Cork - Cork County Council cut off water from 600 homes north Cork when residents there complain of 'unusual tasting' water. Samples taken show a slight excess of chlorine but thought to be a coincidence. No further action taken. (8)

Cork city - ALF phone in several bomb threats to Cork city police, local media and the targeted businesses - fast food establishments in the city centre. Cork Jazz Festival was in full swing so only a limited search was initially carried out but when a suspect device containing wires, a timer and battery was discovered by staff at one of the restaurants 3 hours after the phone threats, the Police immediately emptied the city centre for hours as the army disposal squad carried out a controlled explosion. Presidential campaigner Austin Currie was doing a campaign walkabout at the time and was among those evacuated.

The Army reckons the device might have contained up to 2lbs of explosive. Police are looking for an 'old woman in black clothing' who handed staff the device. (9)

"Like those creatures they seek to protect, the ALF should be put down when they are so desperately and pitifully sick."- journalist Pat Brosnan openly calling for the execution of animal rights activists, Irish Examiner, Oct1, 1990

November, Gardai announce a major two-month probe into increasing ALF activity across the Republic, in particular the posting of over 80 threatening 'poison pen' letters to Coursers by the ALF. Police claim, with absolutely no evidence, they have 'smashed' an ALF campaign to 'intimidate' blood sports enthusiasts. (10)

November, N. Ireland - the Northern Ireland **Hunt Saboteurs Association** announce their formation, stating their intent to use direct action to save foxes from the sadistic clutches of the blood sports fraternity. (11)

Killarney, Co. Kerry - ALF phone in a bomb scare to a Killarney hotel as a disco was in full swing - Gardai evacuate the premises and conduct a search of the building but found nothing. Recent similar bomb threats in Cork prompted quick reaction from the police. It's unclear why the hotel was targeted. (12)

December, Limerick - ALF post turkeys with rat poison injected into them to the Limerick Leader and claim they have poisoned random turkey carcasses in shops across the country. Police are taking the threats 'very seriously'. (13)

Co. Antrim - ALF visit home of man involved in hare coursing and graffiti and throw red paint over his property. (14)

January, Belfast - ALF attack 3 separate fur shops in city centre twice each in January and February. (1)

February, Co. Antrim - 25 Hunt sabs disrupt Killutagh foxhunt twice this month - the first time was marred by violence against the saboteurs who responded by repeating their disruption. (2)

ALF attack two furriers in the centre of Belfast, smashing windows and daubing paint on the walls and gluing up locks. (3)

March, Ulster- ALF set fire to an empty shed at Harriet Vale Poultry farm.10 chickens also rescued from farm. Offices of 'farm' also trashed. This is the farms third attack in 10 years. (4)

Ulster- ALF attack Fairview farm for holding a 'point-to-point' race to raise funds for local hunting club. $1000's in damage done - marquees burned and ripped with knives. (5)

April, Ulster - ALF target a farm on outskirts of Belfast - bales of hay set alight, tractor and potato harvester destroyed. (6)

July, Ulster - ALF attack property of the North Down foxhunt- windows smashed and slogans daubed on property. (7)

Ulster -ALF claim to media that they are in possession of plastic explosives with which to carry on their campaign of economic sabotage. The group state they've had a very successful year with 17 attacks carried out thus far, including recent petrol bomb attacks in Derry, Limavaddy and Cookstown on three pubs for their support of blood sports. (8)

July, Ulster - ALF set fire to a butcher's shop in Newtownards, Belfast. Windows of leather shop also smashed in city centre. (9); ALF set fire to a refrigerated meat truck in CarryDuff. (10)

"Anyone who thinks the meat industry is conducted according to the principals of Mother Theresa would be mistaken"- Beef Baron Larry Goodman at the Beef Tribunal, 1991

Ulster - ALF rescue hens from a factory 'farm' outside Cookstown. (11)

August, Belfast - ALF burn down 3 empty battery farm units and rescue turkeys from a fourth unit. (12)

Belfast - City centre closed off for a day when ALF phone in a firebomb warning, claiming two devices have been planted in J. Braddell & Son's Gun and Fishing shop. One device found and bomb disposal squad make it safe. (13)

Ulster Unionist Party MP J. Taylor urges the State to proscribe the ALF, stating the group's activities could " lead to the loss of human life". This follows an up-tick in ALF activity in the province recently, the latest ALF attack causing $6000 in damages to Lough Cowey fishing club. (14)

September, Ulster - ALF burn out a vehicle and caravan used by Dungannon Coursing Club. (15)

October, Ulster - UK Secretary of State Brian Mawhinney rejects recent UUP MP's appeal to proscribe the ALF under the Emergency Powers Act, stating the police have the required powers to deal with the threat the ALF pose (16); 8 people suspected of being in the ALF arrested and questioned about recent surge of activity - one, David Nelson, held on bail. David is charged with two charges of planting incendiary devices, one charge of planting a petrol bomb underneath a car, criminal damage and 5 counts of arson. He was already on a suspended sentence when arrested so bail was denied. Charges of arson brought against another 4 regarding ten attacks over the last 18 months.

A 50-strong team of detectives had been following the defendants over the previous 3 months before raiding their homes.

"Secret army put terror on shelves"- Irish Independent, Nov. 14, 1991.

November, Ulster - Boots the Chemist remove all bottles of Lucozade from all 14 of their stores in Northern Ireland due to a claim of poisoning by the ALF (Boots are involved in commercial animal experimentation) (17); female hunt saboteur assaulted at Red Hills during a hunt by the Iveagh Harriers. (18)

1992

May, Belfast - **Dave Nelson** gets 3.5 years in the Maze prison for charges of arson and criminal damage to property belonging to blood sports fanatics and factory farms. **Allister Mullen** and **Graeme Cambell** receive 2 years each for similar charges. A team of 50 anti-terrorist officers from the RUC had been assigned to breaking the ALF in Ulster. These three activists, all from the same ALF cell, become Irelands' first animal rights prisoners. (1)

After 6 months inside, Graeme appeals his sentence and the two Judges hearing his appeal considers his two-year sentence "too heavy" and suspend the sentence instead, meaning he is freed immediately. (2)

June, Dublin- Two butchers' shops in Palmerstown have paint thrown over them and slogans daubed on walls. (3)

1993

October - two ICABS activists who were attending a Coursing meet at Cashel incognito are attacked and assaulted by blood sports fanatics and dragged out of the grounds "despite having paid the full price of admission". They went to the Police who themselves went to the Coursing officials and returned the money to the ICABS members. (1)

November, Cork City - An ICABS public meeting on fox hunting is infiltrated by pro-blood sports fanatics and a spokesperson has a chair smashed over his head as the meeting was proceeding. The attack came out of nowhere, with no arguments or heckling leading up to it. The ICABS speaker needed 11 stiches to his skull. As soon as it happened, scores of people immediately left the room. ICABS reckon most of the 90 people who showed up were pro-blood sports and the attack was premeditated. No arrests made. (2)

December, Belfast - City centre McDonalds has windows smashed and locks glued by ALF. (3)

Also in Ulster, encouraged by the HSA, a group of 120 Co. Down farmers form an anti-foxhunting pressure group called **FROTH (Farmers Raising Objection to Hunting)** to campaign against illegal trespassing by local foxhunts. The farmers have had enough of repairing infrastructure damaged by the rampaging huntsmen and their followers.

TWO HUNDRED farmers in Co. Down have endorsed the new group. "If I were to take a herd of bullock...and drive it through where they live, they might see things my way" said one irate farmer.

Interestingly the foxhunts publicly state this to be way more of a threat to their hunting than sabotage. (4)

January, Cork - ALF contact Evening Echo to promise a fresh wave of direct actions against Coursing Clubs across the Country. Police set up 24-hr guard at home of greyhound trainer **Ger McKeenan** after he personally receives death threats from animal rights activists. McKeenan had recently featured in a BBC documentary where he was caught 'blooding' young hounds - i.e., he was throwing live hares to hungry pups to condition ("blood") them to attack hares (1). This is illegal but is widely practiced through the Coursing world as it's the only way the hounds can be trained to chase hares. Similar practices happen in most blood sports. Hares and foxes are not natural prey to these dogs. McKenna later barred for life from the English Greyhound Darby because of this. (1)

Ulster - **Kevin Carson**, a hunt saboteur, starts legal proceedings against a member of the Newry Harriers after being assaulted by him. This is the first civil case against a hunt in Ireland, north or south. (2)

February, Ulster – Animal activists post a wave of incendiary devices to blood sports targets across the UK and Republic of Ireland. (3)

March, Co. Tipperary - ALF post parcel bomb to HQ of the Irish Coursing Club in Tipperary. Recent revelations on TV of the Irish Coursing Club feeding hares strapped to poles to hungry greyhounds inflames public opinion. (4)

May, Ulster - ALF set fire to a building belonging to Queens University Psychology lab, presumably for experimenting on animals. (5)

July, Ulster- ALF target house of the Master of the County Down staghounds but attack his father's house by mistake, himself a retired hunts master. (6)

Ulster - the Belfast Telegraph report that Northern Irish hunt saboteurs have been teaching Republic of Ireland activists the art of hunt sabotage. Dublin activists have also been out sabbing with their counterparts in the North to gain first-hand experience in the techniques of effective sabotage.

40 activists from across the Republic attend a weekend seminar on hunt sabotage in preparation for the upcoming foxhunting season in September. Up to 100 activists intend sabbing hunts all over the South. (7)

Ulster - Activists claim to have sent 3 parcel bombs in the post to individuals involved in the Game and Country Fair at Shanes castle. (8)

The local Free Presbyterian Church (AKA The 'Wee Free's' / Ian Paisleys lot) also oppose the Fair, but only because its being held on Sunday, the Lords Day of rest.

August, Belfast - **Nina Wilson**, a Belfast-based animal rights campaigner and hunt saboteur, denies accusations she planted a firebomb in Parsons and Parsons hunting shop. Nina is held on remand and questioned about this and other recent ALF actions. Police claim to have found fibres of Nina's' gloves in the pocket of the coat the device was apparently left in. They also found an open box of firelighters at the suspects house when they raided it. (!)

Nina is acquitted by the Jury and vows to continue fighting peacefully for animal rights. (9)

October, Cork - Police contacted by a major shipping company when they receive a parcel in the post with stickers on the parcel promoting animal welfare. The company believed it to be a bomb as they had been attacked by the ALF recently over their involvement in the live export trade. When police inspected the suspect device, they discovered it was merely a campaign video sent to them by **Compassion in World Farming.** They hoped the Companies' Director's would watch the video to persuade from further involvement in the trade. (10)

September - first wave of foxhunt sabotage begins in the Republic of Ireland, with hunts in Dublin and Galway receiving regular attention from saboteurs. Violence from mounted huntsmen at second **Galway Blazer**s foxhunt sabotage, with activists being whipped and horses used as battering rams against sabs. Nevertheless, sabotage successful and hunt left confused and, ahem, 'outfoxed'. (11)

1995

January, Galway- major incident at **Galway Blazers** foxhunt when the hunt turns on sabs and engage in a prolonged, and premeditated, attack on sabs, trying to overturn vehicles, damaging cars belonging to the sabs and physically assaulting any sab they could get their hands on. Local hunt supporters join in the assault. Sabs have camera equipment stolen. Most of this takes place in full view of the 6 police present. The cops refuse to intervene or assist sabs, and refuse to present evidence to the DPP*, stonewalling the attempted prosecution against the Blazers by the saboteurs. (1)
*** DPP** = Dept. of Public Prosecutions AKA *Don't Prosecute the Privileged*

Belfast - ALF plant firebombs in Woolworths and Habitat in city centre. British army bomb disposal diffuse both devices. (2)

Co. Carlow and Co. Roscommon - ALF release hares captured and caged by local Coursing Clubs. Pat Phelan from ICABS yet again vocally condemns these actions in the media but is then himself criticised by groups like the Alliance for Animal Rights and CACS for endlessly condemning non-violent, if illegal, direct action. AFAR and CACS welcome the ALF's actions and describe ICABS as out of touch with the realities of the struggle for animal rights. (3)

July, Co. Down - ALF post a hoax bomb to a live animal exporter, Mr. Sam Smyth of Crossgar, Downpatrick. A suspect device in a jiffy bag was dealt with by bomb disposal. Mr Smyth has received numerous threats in the recent past from animal militants and police advised him and all others involved in the export trade to be on alert. (4)

October – Northern Irish Saboteurs hit the Oriel Foxhunt and are attacked by a mob of hunt support – their vehicle was surrounded and attacked, and equipment was stolen. (5)

1996

March, Ulster - RUC inform Gardai that an ex-loyalist paramilitary-turned-ALF activist is planning to bomb any port involved in live animal export, north or south of the border. Gardai heighten security in ports across the country as a result. (1)

Belfast hunt saboteurs focus on sabotaging the County Down Staghunt, a particularly obnoxious variant of hunting and one of only two of its kind (the other being in the Republic of Ireland). These Stags are bred for the sole purpose of hunting, so-called 'bagged' hunting. A dozen vehicles packed with sabs blockaded the road outside the stag farm all day and prevented the hunt. The convoy of saboteurs left when dusk fell. Police arrested 9 Saboteurs under the brand-new Criminal Justice Act but the charges were all later dropped. This was a common outcome for activists charged under the CJA due to the law's vagueness and unreasonable nature. (2)

August - UK and Irish ALF both phone in calls to media again threatening sabotage on any port involved in live export. Cork port singled out as first to be attacked should this trade resume. (Live exports had been put on hold due to the outbreak of Mad Cow disease (BSE)). (3)

ALF also name specific companies they are targeting. These companies hire Private Investigators to track animal rights activists. (4)

Media report ALF activists suspected of being among the recent influx of New Age Travellers from Britain fleeing the Thatcherite Junta....Zero evidence offered for this. (5)

"Fiery revenge of 'unhappy hooker'"- Sunday Independent, Sept. 6, 1996.

September, Cork - A live export ship has a petrol bomb thrown on to its deck in what police initially think is an ALF attack. Turns out it was done by a local prostitute and her 'John' in a dispute over payment with some of the crew on board. Fire quickly brought under control. Bomb narrowly misses tons of very flammable hay on the ship. Sailors, eh? can't take 'em anywhere. (5)

Media report that the UK police are still sharing details on UK animal activists with Gardai. (6)

1997

MAKING PLANS FOR NIGEL - January, Co. Waterford - local saboteurs are joined by 23 sabs from the UK and descend on the annual foxhunt at Kilmeaden. Gardai get wind of arrival of UK sabs and stop their transit van *en route* to the hunt meet point - cudgels and whips confiscated from the saboteurs. Despite this the day quickly becomes violent and a battle between balaclava'd sabs and hunt support becomes known locally as the **Battle of Houghtons Cross**. Stones, clubs, whips and boots used by both sides despite a strong police presence. Five sabs are injured, one hospitalised but later self -discharges. (1) One UK sab was arrested for possession of an offensive weapon - a whip - and bailed but never returned to face charges. Judge orders a bench warrant for his arrest. (2) Hunt left in disarray. ICABS condemn the saboteurs' actions.

The **hunts Master, Nigel Cox, is a convicted criminal** following an incident at a hunt in the UK in 1985 where he shot at an occupied hunt sabs van, blowing a hole in the vehicle's radiator, attacked a saboteur with the gun butt and damaged a camera. For all this he received a 3-month *suspended* sentence* (3). The Irish Master of Foxhounds spokesman J. Norton called on the State to be more stringent with animal rights protesters yet fails to mention Cox's previous criminal history. (4) * *one wonders what sentence from the Courts a hunt saboteur might have received if he/she had shot up an occupied hunt vehicle. More than a three-month suspended sentence methinks....*

March, Co. Kilkenny - Ten hunt saboteurs get in an altercation with supporters of the North Kilkenny foxhunt at Gathabawn. Police are called to the scene - The Saboteurs had successfully split the hunting pack using the 'Gizmo'* and horn calls, enraging the hunt who blockaded the sabs in their vehicle for the 20 minutes it took the police to arrive. The hunt support disappeared as soon as they saw the police. (5)

> *A Gizmo is a tape-recorder attached to a small amplifier – when the pre-recorded sound of hounds 'on cry' is played through it, the real hounds are drawn magnetically to the sound, thinking other dogs have found quarry.*

April, Co. Cork - **Compassion in World Farming**, a group not usually known for its surreptitious activity, sneak a camera into a formal tour of the Teagasc pig breeding research facility to record the suffering of the animals there. The pigs are kept in tiny stalls and tethered by rope. The research centre investigates ways to squeeze more and more out of the animals so farmers can maximise profit. CIWF use the video as part of their 'Freedom for Irish Sows' campaign. (6)

August, Co. Meath - Hunt saboteurs manage to secretly film the digging out of a fox gone to ground, an illegal act and one formally condemned by the hunting fraternity, though commonplace. The dig-out takes place at the request of the notorious Ward Union hunt and causes public uproar. (7)

"It is agonizing to read about the way that pigs are borne aloft by hooks, screaming as their throats are cut. Even the strongest nerves of the most hardened workers are shaken by the experience. There is something about that shriek…." Christopher Hitchens.

1998

February, Ulster – Anonymous animal activists post a letter bomb to a solicitor's office in Lurgan, Co. Armagh. Solicitor involved in local hunt. Device fails to go off. (1)

1999

February, Co. Carlow - 8 sabs manage to sabotage a local foxhunt in Bagenalstown so successfully that the hunt abandon chasing any foxes and turn on the sabs instead. Sabs withdrew in 2 vehicles, but one vehicle gets hemmed in by 3 range rovers full of outraged huntsmen. An altercation ensued, with one sab getting dragged out of his vehicle and the car keys stolen. The huntsmen then disappeared. The keys were later found nearby on a wall. Sabs shaken but unharmed. (1)

2000 - October, Co. Offlay - ALF release 30 Hares from cages at Edenderry Coursing club. Pat Phelan of ICABS condemns the action. Bernie Wright of the Alliance for Animal Rights welcomes it. (1)

2001

January, Co. Galway, - Irelands third largest Coursing club has all its hares stolen by another Coursing club, forcing them to cancel their meet. Untrustworthy lot, those Coursers. (1)

Co. Offaly -Police called to scene of confrontation between 10 saboteurs and the Streamstown Harriers. (2)

December, Limerick - **ARAN*** and **CALF*** activists storm the Ryan hotel who have leased a room to Barnardos furriers for the weekend. The 5 activists locked themselves together in the hotel lobby at 6pm and began chanting anti-fur slogans. Meanwhile activists from around the country jammed the phonelines of the hotel to further drive the message home. Stink bombs were also set off. No arrests were made. (3)

*ARAN - Animal rights Action Network (now defunct); **CALF** - Campaign Against Leather and Fur

2002

November, Co. Meath - a male fox hound belonging to a Country Meath Hunt was rescued and rehomed. This dog, when seen by a vet, was covered in ticks, fleas and lice, and had lumps all over his body. The dog has now settled in happily with his new family. (1)

"Let's just say I would not like to get on the wrong side of those people"- pro-hunting campaigner on the Fox-Hunting fraternity, Irish Independent, Nov. 8, 2000. Do they have a 'right' side?

2003

January, Co. Meath - 4 anti-hunt demonstrators from the Association of Hunt Saboteurs are attacked by a vile mob of blood sports fanatics at Kells, Co. Meath. Banners are torn down and punches aimed at them by the enraged mob. Police refuse to take any action, either during the assault or afterwards. (1)
February, Co. Offlay - ALF release 1000 mink into the wild from a mink fur farm in Laois. Extensive video footage also taken and sent to above-ground animal rights groups for further dissemination. (2)

June, Co. Kildare - ALF destroy 40 squirrel traps that were set up by the EPA and the Zoological Dept. of Trinity College, Dublin. (3)

Dublin - Circus Vegas, had their signs pasted with 'Cancelled' stickers and other signs were removed. One large sign was sprayed with the initials 'A.L.F.' (4)

Co. Waterford - **John Tierney** is sentenced to jail for two months for breach of the peace during a foxhunt by blowing a foghorn during the hunt proceedings, frightening the bejasus out of everyone's horses apparently. The Judge presiding over the case states he would have understood if people had caught him by the "scruff of his neck" at the time due to the shock he caused. (5)

John immediately appeals the sentence and wins. (6)

July, Co. Dublin -communique from the ALF - ' Circus Vegas was paid a visit by the ALF during its stay in Celbridge. Direction signs and advertising posters were removed. Large metal signs had red paint poured over them and one of their trucks had brake-fluid thrown across it. Signs were pasted around the Cellbridge area, by the ALF, informing local residents of the reasons why they should boycott this circus.'(7)

2004

January, Co. Kildare - ALF rescue 2 hens from a factory farm. The owner bizarrely claims the hens would probably have died 'within half an hour' after being rescued. He fails to explain how or why. The activists name the birds Ginger and Rocky after two characters in the recent 'Chicken Run' movies. (1)

Four anti-hunt protesters are once again attacked by members of the Meath Hunt in full view of police who remained passive throughout the attack. (2)

April, Meath - The AIB bank formally withdraw all financial and moral support for the Ward Union Stag hunt following media pressure from the Association of Hunt Saboteurs. (3)

June, Co. Meath - communique from the ALF - "The Vegas Circus had an unexpected visit from the ALF last night. Before their performances even started all their promotional and directional signs were removed and destroyed. These signs were mostly on main roads, some being over eight foot long."(4)

July - Dublin - Activists from AFAR are assaulted by circus goers as they handed out leaflets outside the Circus Vegas in Castleknock. Two were punched to the ground. Police and activists toured venue after assault but couldn't find assailants. Besides hunt sabotage, protesting a circus is a sure-fire way to be punched. (5)

October, Limerick - ALF damage huge billboards inside Greyhound stadium for its support of Coursing. (6)

Mallow, Co. Cork - On the opening night of the Dare Devils circus in Mallow, ALF activists completely remove and destroy huge billboards and poster boards advertising the circus. (7)

November, Dublin - The ALF entered Shelbourne Park Racing track undetected in broad daylight and blocked up the toilets in the main building. This action was in protest at the slaughter of thousands of Greyhounds at the hands of Bord na gCon*. (8)

*Bord na gCon are a semi-state body that regulate, and finance, the Greyhound industry. This year (2021), the taxpayer subsided this cruel, dying 'sport' to the tune of $19.2 million Euro. Next year they're getting $17.6 million.

December, Dublin - Signs advertising Fossett's circus in Booterstown were pasted with 'cancelled' stickers. (9)

Monknewtown, Slane - ALF rescue ten turkeys from a Russels breeding farm. Farmer denies raid ever happened. (10)

Kildare - Eight chickens were rescued from Enfield Broiler Breeders in Allenwood South. (11)

Limerick - ALF scale high fenced walls and enter a wild bird holding cell in Limerick city. These wild birds would have eventually being either bred or sold on. ALF open the cages and free all birds. (12)

2005

January - ALF contact national media and repeat their threats of sabotage, including arson, against all who actively support Coursing. (1)

Co. Tipperary - an ALF cell attacked the hare-coursing venue Powerstown Park Racecourse in Clonmel. In a two-hour operation, ALF members spread nails and tacks on the field of the racecourse and at the entrance to the venue. Several incendiary devices were also placed around the racecourse. An ALF spokesperson said further attacks were planned on this venue in the run up to the National Hare Coursing Finals. The spokesperson said that war had been declared on animal abusers in Ireland. (2)

February, Co. Dublin - Two large twenty-foot-long signs advertising the Fingal Harriers Hunt were removed from flyovers in County Dublin. (3)

May, Co. Dublin - Bird shooters arrived back to their cars to find their locks had been superglued and paintwork had been keyed with the initials "ALF". This is the second time they have received attention from the ALF. (4)

Dublin - "exotic" butchers in Terenure has its locks filled with superglue gel; butcher's van in Ballinteer was covered in paint stripper. (5)

Dublin - A fishing/shooting store in Lucan was targeted by the ALF. The shutters, which display a badly painted scene of fishing and shooting, "have now been artistically altered with bright red paint displaying the initials 'ALF' ". Locks also glued. (6)

June, Kildare -Over 70 Circus posters torn down, Dare Devil circus vandalised; A farmer's field that the Circus were due to use had its entrance gate locks glued up. (7)

July - national paper Sunday Independent report ALF activists have begun spying on senior employees of two major animal research companies in Dublin (Glaxo Smith-Kline and Myeth Co.). (8)

Dublin - house of a well-known fur shop owner in Rathfarnham was visited. A Volvo car was covered in paint stripper. (9)

August, Limerick -Three goats removed from a Traveller halting site in Limerick city. The animals were placed in a safe, secure home away from the miserable life they had up until then. (10)

Dublin - Two cars containing fishing gear were damaged whilst they were left parked at the harbour. (11)

October, Dublin - Circus posters promoting Circus Vegas destroyed. (12)

Dublin - A bookies shop in County Dublin has its locks superglued 'in protest at the exploitation and abuse of both race-horses and Greyhounds for racing.'(13)

November, Co. Meath - ALF damage vehicle and property of Irelands only exporter of the European Common frog for use in experiments throughout Europe. The frog farm owner, Denis McCarthy, expressed dismay at the attack in the media, stating he had been in touch with the ALF via an intermediary and "I was under the impression they would leave me alone as I'm winding my business down" he said. He was wrong it seems. (14)

December, Dublin - - ALF pay a visit to Barnardos Furriers. Red paint was poured all over the locks and shutters. On the same night, ALF members paid a visit to a butcher's shop near Stephens Green and poured red paint through the letter box. Also, a nearby hunting supply shop has locks glued and its shop front was redecorated in red paint. (15)

Limerick - ALF daub red paint all over the doors and deface the signs of a hunting store in Limerick city. (16)

January, Waterford - ALF report they have been systematically removing hundreds of badger snares set by the Dept. of Agribusiness over the last 6 months. (1)

March, Dublin - In the early hours of March 28th the ALF visited the home of Caroline Barnardo and paint stripped her car. Caroline Barnardo owns Barnardo Furriers, Dublin's oldest, and most frequently attacked, fur shop. (2)

April, Co. Dublin - Fossett's Circus in Leixlip have their signs removed and destroyed. On the same night a Hunting & Fishing shop in Lucan has its locks glued. and 'ALF' sprayed across the front of the shop. (3)

May, Dublin - 100 circus signs belonging to Duffy's Circus are destroyed. (4)

June, Dublin- more circus signs defaced and destroyed. (5)

August, Co. Waterford - circus signs destroyed in Tramore. "This is in retaliation for beating up a 76-year-old woman protestor recently." said the ALF communique in reference to a recent assault by circus thugs on a protestor at a previous location. (6)

Dublin - Over sixty circus advertising signs are destroyed belonging to Circus Sydney during their stay in Balbriggan. This circus abandoned a monkey for a week in a van without food, also this circus has attacked protestors on four separate occasions. (7)

October, Dublin - 4 large advertising signs for the Ward Union Point to Point are destroyed with paint; Over 60 signs belonging to Circus Hoffenberg erected on the Navan Road are removed and destroyed.(8)

Co. Meath - Over 40 Advertising signs for The Royal Russian Circus are destroyed or removed. (9)

Co. Carlow - A Bookmakers in County Carlow has its locks glued in retaliation for the cruelty involved in the racing Industry. 'ALF' sprayed on its windows; Butchers shop belonging to an abattoir owner has its walls covered with red paint. This is the third time this premises has been damaged. (10)

December, Dublin - hunting and shooting shop has its shutters covered in paint. (11)

Dublin - ALF visit Barnardo furriers and Rohu furriers on two occasions and all their locks are superglued shut, all locks have to be replaced; Also, one furrier has some 'redecoration' work done on their shop front. (12)

2007

January, Co. Meath - Shooter's car paint-stripped, and windscreen wipers and locks superglued. (1)

Dublin city - animal rights activists glue the locks on four Dublin fur stores - A Store is Born, Rohu Furs, Barnardo's Furriers and Sydney Vards Furriers are all targeted. Again. (2)

Co. Westmeath - Ten unattended hunt vehicles were paint stripped. Thousands of euros in damage caused. (3)

Co. Kildare - A vehicle belonging to a fisherman had brake fluid poured over it and its locks glued while he pulled fish from a river. (4)

February, Kildare- A butcher's shop has its door locks glued shut and a Hunting shop has its locks superglued for the seventh time. (5)

Co. Carlow - A Fox hunt has its roadside signs advertising its annual Point to Point destroyed and removed. (6)

March, Co. Galway - The Galway Blazers Hunt has one of their vehicles damaged, with tyres slashed and windscreen broken at their meet at Curley's Pub. (7)

March, Dublin - city butchers shop daubed with paint. (8)

Kildare - meat van paint stripped. (9)

April, Wexford - The Royal Russian Circus has 60 advertising boards destroyed in County Wexford. (10)

May, Dublin - 60 signs advertising the circus are destroyed; Three of Dublin's fur shops-- Bernardo's, Sydney Vard and Rohu-- have their locks glued and red paint poured on them. (11)

Kildare - A hunting and shooting shop in County Kildare has its locks glued (yet again). (12)

June, Dublin - 30 Circus advertising signs for Circus VEGAS are removed or destroyed in Maynooth/Blanchardstown area. (13)

July, Dublin - locks of a Butchers shop in North Dublin are super-glued. (14)

August, Dublin - 5 bookies and 2 butchers' shops have their locks glued; 3 fur shops have locks glued and slogans spray painted on their shutters; Trinity College has one of its entrances spray-painted with slogans such as 'vivisection is scientific fraud', 'we're aware of your animal cruelty' and 'animal abusers'. (15)

September, Dublin - Dublin ALF carry out an action against Howard Vard (owner of Sydney Vards fur shop). His home is visited, and his black BMW is destroyed with paint stripper. (16)

October, Co. Meath - Circus Vegas in Fairyhouse is the target of the ALF when about 50 advertising signs are destroyed. (17)

2008

January, Dublin - Anti-fur protestors launch paint attacks on two Dublin city centre clothing shops over the Christmas holiday. Red gloss paint thrown across the front of The Turet and the Harlequin stores (1)

Forty Circus Vegas advertising signs destroyed, and eight-gun club signs removed or graffitied. (2)

March, Co. Laois - communique from ALF - "last weekend, the Animal Liberation Front visited Ireland's largest fur farm - Vasa Ltd, in Co. Laois. The ALF made their way through the locked gate in a matter of seconds, and then the real fun started...A quick scan of the area showed that the sheds were enclosed in an area secured by corrugated steel. No problem - a huge hole was then cut into this, the wire mesh behind it snipped, and the hedgerow behind that was then cleared - to allow the Mink easy access to the river running beside this concentration camp. Graffiti was sprayed all around the place, including the signature 'ALF' calling card.300 breeding cards were removed from one of the sheds, and then destroyed. Moving onto the next shed, 300 Mink were liberated and were then guided to freedom, before the ALF disappeared into the darkness. It was unbearable to have to leave the others behind. Una and Michael Heffernan are responsible for murdering over 45,000 Mink on this death camp every year. It's time to make them pay for this."(3)

May, Dublin - communique from the ALF - "fur shops such as Sydney Vard furriers and 'Barnardo's' were spray painted with slogans such as 'FUR IS MURDER', 'FUR SCUM' and of course 'A.L.F.' and the locks were glued while 'rohu' furs had their locks glued. La Cave' restaurant who sell the cruel 'foie gras' duck/goose liver dish was also targeted with spray paint. Trinity college, who openly engage in vivisection, had their science entrance sprayed with 'vivisection is scientific fraud', 'free the animals', 'vivisection-lies' and, 'ALF'. Also, a local tattoo parlour, who up until recently before being sold to a new, loving home held a python snake in a small tank and cruel conditions in their studio, had their front window spray painted and their locks glued as pay back for the snake."(4)

June, Dublin- over 100 Duffy's circus posters removed and destroyed around Dublin. (5)

October, Waterford - Fox killers have their vehicles damaged as they dig out foxes with terriers and lurchers. (6)

2009

February - the ALF, in collaboration with the Coalition to Abolish the Fur Trade (CAFT), send DVD's containing footage taken by the ALF from inside all 6 fur farms in the Republic of Ireland to every elected TD in the State, exposing the cruelty of the $2 million per year industry and urging they ban this vicious trade. Footage shows animals in distress displaying symptoms of psychosis. (1)

July, Dublin -communique from the ALF - " Duffy's Circus targeted. Trucks and cars were sabotaged, wires cut, locks glued, and property was damaged. A clear message was painted for them, so they would know the reason behind this attack: STOP USING ANIMALS; later in the month the circus was hit again - 2 trucks and 5 cars spray painted, and locks welded,1 van treated with paint remover; Also, two anglers' vehicles had their locks glued tight as they were hauling bodies from the water."(2)

August - a hunting and fishing shop in Lucan is spray painted and has its locks glued shut. The messages read 'A.L.F.: STOP SELLING DEATH' and the ALF symbol. (3)

September, Dublin - Ninety AUSTRALIAN SUPER CIRCUS SYDNEY advertising billboards were destroyed. This circus, formerly part of Circus Vegas, is notorious for attacking protestors and for releasing animals on to major roads as advertising stunts. (4)

October, Dublin - Over 20 premises including pet shops, bookmakers, fur shops, butchers and fast-food restaurants spray painted, and locks glued. (5)

December, Dublin - 1 McDonalds,3 butchers,1 pet shop,1 fur shop and 6 bookmakers all have their locks glued. (7)

Dublin - a **NARA** protester outside furriers A Star is Born in Dublin city is assaulted by the Shop owner, 61-year-old **Marie Murphy**. Murphy violently shoved into campaigner **Laura Broxson** from behind, pushing her into the gutter. Laura got up and shoved Murphy back and was struck in the mouth as a result.

In an act of stunning hypocrisy, Murphy then called Laura a Nazi, adding "I've been wanting to do that for ages". A person whose trade consists of caging millions of animals in what are essentially concentration camps before gassing them calls someone opposed to that a Nazi....Murphy also accused the 4 demonstrators present of vandalising her shop recently.

Murphy was found guilty at Trial in 2011 and fined 500 Euro for assault causing injury. She should have received another 6 months for calling Laura a Nazi (8).

Laura continued with a Civil case for personal injury against Murphy and was awarded 9000 Euro in 2013. Murphy also had to pay Court costs, which typically run into four figures.

2010

January, Dublin - a KFCs in Bray is attacked by a new group calling itself **RAGE - Resistance Against Global Evil**. Bricks chucked at windows and door, but no significant damage done. (1)

February, Belfast - a self-described 'lone wolf' activist of the ALF & several tubes of super glue, visits the following premises - 2 butchers' shops, 2 bookmakers' shops and 1 hunting/fishing tackle shop. The locks of these premises are thoroughly glued. (2)

March, Belfast - locks glued up at a butcher and bookmakers' shops. (3)

July, Dublin - Duffy's circus posters slashed in Goatstown.(4)

August, Belfast - ALF glue up locks of 6 shops including butchers, bookmakers, and hunting stores. (5)

September, Dublin - 40 posters advertising the Super Australian Circus destroyed; later in the month the home of the owner of Barnardo's furriers was attacked with red paint and gates chained and padlocked. (6)

Belfast - 2 Butchers shops and 2 Betting shops have their doors & window shutters and are made unopenable for the next day's 'trade'. (7)

Kildare - 40 more Super Australian Circus posters destroyed in Maynooth. (8)

Donegal - ALF open 1000 cages in a mink farm near Ardara, freeing 5000 mink. The animals were due to be killed in the coming weeks. (9)

"Sand in the petrol tank means that deliveries going nowhere/ when a new death shop opens up make sure you're the first person to be there/ when the circus comes to town/ remember what goes up must come down" Conflict, 'This is the ALF'

2011

March, Dublin - Letter left at family home of Barnardo's fur shop owner, stating simply DROP FUR OR DROP DEAD. Family car covered in paint stripper, note pinned with a knife to a bike owned by a staff member asking they withdraw from the trade or expect repercussions. Staff members home address included in note. (1)

LEONARD IS A MORAN - November, Mayo, Ballina- Four NARA activists hold a small, peaceful picket outside the premises of two adjoining Companies that experiment on animals- Ovagen and Charles Rivers Laboratories. The CEO of Ovagen, ex-rugby player Leonard Moran, emerged out of a hedge wielding a hammer and punched activist **Laura Broxson** in the face. "I have been tormented by this individual (Laura). She's like a little terrier in and around my house" he pleaded to the Judge. This was NARA's tenth demonstration at the Labs. Moran explained that his assault on Laura wouldn't have even earned him "a yellow card on the rugby field". In any case, Moran stated to the police he "didn't care if they protested 365 days a year", it didn't bother him and that's why he ran through a hedge with a hammer in his hand to get at them. He had also recently spent one million Euro on security for his business premises. (2)

Moran was found guilty and put on probation. Laura then pursued a Civil case against him and was awarded 10,000 Euro plus costs. True to form, Moran paid only 5000 Euro to her lawyers and nothing to Laura.

April, Dublin- Barnardo's and Rohu furriers and various butchers' shops in city centre have their locks glued; Also in Dublin, a car with pro-hunting stickers on it is damaged. (3)

Dublin - **Neil Lenoach**, aged 24, becomes Republic of Irelands first person to be jailed for animal-rights related offences, of a unique kind, when he is imprisoned for 3 years for launching a pepper-spray attack on customers and staff at a KFC in Bray last February.

LEN WOLF - Lenoach entered the restaurant in a balaclava carrying a baton and pepper spray and immediately began spraying the two customers and one staff member present. Police arrived quickly and arrested Leonach as he made his way out the emergency exit. Although a violent and unusual act, it was apparently motivated by the genuine distress Neil felt about the way society treats animals, particularly in the fast-food industry. Lenoachs mother stated in the media that Neil had long been interested in animal welfare and was tormented by thoughts of animals suffering. Neil's' Solicitor argued he suffered from mild Asperger's and urged it to be a mitigating factor but the Judge dismissed this argument. (4)

Neil has no association with the ALF or any other animal rights groups.

2012

January, Co. Meath – vehicles belonging to Fingal Harriers hunt club damaged. Tyres slashed and bodywork scratched. (1)

March, Co. Meath - unattended hunt vehicles once again damaged with paint stripper by ALF. (2)

2013

May, Dublin - Locks glued at Barnardo Furs, Rohu Furs, and Sydney Vard Furriers. (1)
October, Dublin - over 50 Duffy's posters destroyed by ALF; Also, all 4 of Dublin's fur retail shops have locks glued and paint thrown over them. 'Fur Scum' daubed on shutters; 50 large Duffy's circus posters destroyed. (2)

2014

January, Co. Down -Co. Down - new group of hunt saboteurs close down local hunt from even starting by simply turning up and freaking the hunt out. The hunt claimed to be outraged by their presence and insisted the saboteur's attendance was "contravening the rules outlined in the Parades Commission for lawful assembly". The huntsmen's civil rights were being denied but at the same time "not a day's hunting has been lost" they fumed. (1)

June, Co. Laois - ALF visit Vasa fur farm in Laois. Gates D-locked and entrance pillars spray painted. (2)

October, Dublin, (Santry, Blancherstown & Ballymun) - Over 40 Duffy's circus posters destroyed. (3)

Dublin - $7000 worth of fur coats in Harvey Nichols shop, Dundrum, destroyed with chewing gum. Chew on that! (4)

November, Dublin - Barnardos, Sydney Vale, Paula Rowan and Rohu fur shops all have locks glued and walls spray painted by the ALF on Halloween night. Activists presumably dressed as animals. (5)

December - new activist group called the **Hunt Retribution Group** attack pubs who host fox hunt meets. Pubs in Louth, Meath, the Midlands, and Cork damaged. (6)

2015

May, Dublin city - animal activists from several groups including the **National Animal Rights Association** enter the 'Ka-Shing' restaurant in Wicklow St. during opening hours and remove 9 live lobsters from the fish tank in the window display. The lobsters are driven to the beach where they are released into the sea. This is the world's first successful open lobster rescue! (1)

above - ***Man bites dog? NO! Woman Pinches Lobster!***

Laura Broxson *and another activist reach in to rescue the lobsters as diners looked on, Ka Shing restaurant, Dublin, 2015. This was the* ***world's first recorded daylight successful lobster open rescue****. Someone tell Norris McWhirter. Stock image.*

2016

January - A disruption of toilet facilities at the Pillo Hotel in County Meath was carried out due to the hotel hosted for the Ward Union Hunt Ball. (1)

March, Dublin, Granard- All 80 (expensive) circus signs for the Renz circus destroyed. (2)

2017

no recorded actions

2018

Donegal - four NARA activists manage to gain access to a fur farm in Gleties, Donegal, by pretending to the staff that they were simply lost tourists. They asked for directions, got chatting and then casually asked if they could have a look inside the farm, out of curiosity. Their hidden cameras captured the squalid conditions the 1-year-old mink are caged in. The action was part of an ongoing anti-fur campaign by NARA. (1)

above -*Hunters engage with a Galway Hunt Sab West of Ireland, circa 2019. Stock image.*

2019

July, Co. Westmeath - 80 '**Meat the Victims'** activists' trespass onto a pig farm in Raharny and document the cruelty and horror taking place. This was the group's first action. No damage was done, and no animals rescued but the media ran with it. Predictably faux-outraged and hypocritical reaction from the Irish Farmers Association. (1)

April, Co. Laois, Vicarstown - ALF D-lock gates and spray paint slogans on walls of premises of a fur farm. (2)

"It's a rough, frantic, and sometimes brutal business, a world of blood and bone and knife and stench. One contractor told me 'You need to be half-savage to do it.'" Author Fintin O'Toole on the Irish meat industry, from 'We Don't know Ourselves.' 2021

2020

January, Co. Antrim - 40 activists from Meat the Victims entered a farm in Ballymena, Northern Ireland on Tuesday morning and rescued a pig The group posted live video footage of their actions whilst on the farm as well as photos of dead and dying animals. During the visit, which started at 4.30 in the morning, the group identified one injured pig that they wanted to 'save' and took it from the farm. Police officers did attend the scene but later said no criminal action had taken place. (1)

above – *Meat The Victims rescue a pig from a farm in Ballymena, Northern Ireland.*

February, - Downpatrick, Northern Ireland - Politicians, Farmers, and the local branch of the League Against Cruel Sports (LACS) meet up to discuss how best to keep unwanted hunters from wrecking property and potentially spreading disease like TB across the countryside. LACS are providing practical legal advice and support to farmers who have had enough of roaming gangs of stupidly dressed foxhunters tearing up land and damaging infrastructure and threatening anyone who questions them. One hunt supporter was recently arrested for intimidating behaviour against a farmer who asked he get off his land. (3)

June, Co. Armagh - ALF take 35 ducks being bred as shooting targets from Castledillon Estate and rehome them away from the guns of psychopaths. Two hunt huts on the Estate also destroyed. (4)

2021 - June, East Ireland - two magpies released from cruel Larsen trap and trap destroyed. (1)

September -location unknown – three wooden hunting towers smashed up by ALF (2)

REFERENCE LIST FOR DIARY OF ACTIONS:

1964

(1) 'Hares escape so meeting is off', Evening Herald, Dublin, Jan.25,1964, p3

1982

(1) 'blood sports', Evening Herald, Dublin, Jan.6, p.12,1983.
(2) 'The Anglo-Irish connection', HOWL magazine, Spring 1983, no. 24, p.8.
(3) 'Second slogan attack on furrier', Belfast Telegraph, Oct.9, p.5,1982
(4) 'fur trade protest', Belfast Telegraph, Nov.27,1982, p.24.
(5) 'Group News', HOWL magazine, Spring 1983, no. 24, p.6.
(6) 'Irish Sabotage', HOWL magazine, Spring 1983, no. 24, p.12.

1983

(1) 'Group News', HOWL magazine, Spring 1983, no. 24, p.6.
(2) 'Group News', HOWL magazine, Spring 1983, no. 24, p.6.
(3) 'Group News', HOWL magazine, Spring 1983, no. 24, p.6.
(4) ALF SG Diary of actions, Dec #8, p.11,1983. (UK)
(5) 'Group News', HOWL magazine, Spring 1984, no. 27, p.13.

1984

(1) ALF SG Diary of Actions, Newsletter 11, April, p.10,1984. (UK)
(2) 'Guinea pigs rescued', Evening Herald, Dublin, June 16, p.2,1984; ALF SG Diary of actions, #13, Oct.p.12,1984. (UK)
(3) ALF SG Diary of actions, #13, Oct.p.12,1984. (UK)
(4) ALF SG Diary of actions, #13, Oct.p.13,1984. (UK)
(5)
(6) ALF SG Diary of actions, #14, p.3,1984. (UK)
(7) ALF SG Diary of actions, #14, p.4,1984. (UK)
(8) Jim Flanagan, 'Hare coursing protesters clash with police', Belfast Telegraph, No.14, p.23,1984.
(9) Noeleen Dowling, 'Poisoned shampoo scare in stores', Irish Press, Dublin, Dec.01,1984
(10) William Dillon, 'Christmas turkey poison scare in three cities', Irish Independent, Dublin, Dec.13, p.1,1984.
(11) Irish Independent, Dublin, December 28th, p.3,1984.
(12) 'Fence damaged on eve of hare coursing event', Belfast Telegraph, Dec.1, p.1,1984.
(13) ' 90 hares freed in attack on club', Evening Echo (Cork), Dec.19, p.15,1984.

1985

(1) 'Campaign against butchers', Evening Herald, Jan.28, p.8,1985.

(2) Peter Cluskey, 'Butchers see red after daubing!', Evening Echo, Feb 21, p.1,1985.

(3) ALF SG Diary of Actions #16, p. 16,1985. (UK)

(4) ALF SG Diary of Actions #16, p. 16,1985. (UK)

(5) ALF SG Diary of Actions #16, p. 19,1985. (UK)

(6) ALF SG Diary of Actions #16, p.21,1985. (UK)

(7) ALF SG Diary of Actions #21, p. 16,1985. (UK)

(8) 'A statue that's not moving', Irish Press, Dublin.Aug.28, p. 3,1985.

(9) Dan Collins, 'Coursing club raided by Animal Liberation Front', Irish Examiner, Cork, Sept.28, p.7,1985.

(10) 'The course roughed up', Irish Examiner, Cork, Nov.5, p.19,1985.

(11) Jim Cluskey 'Coursing Grounds Attacked', Evening Echo, Cork, Dec.10, P.16,1985; ALF SG Diary of Actions, #19, p.28.

(12) ALF SG Diary of Actions, #15, p.3,1985. (UK)

1986

(1) ALF SG Diary of Actions, #15, p.4,1986. (UK)

(2) ALF SG Diary of Actions, #15, p.4,1986. (UK)

(3) 'Sabotage fails to halt flashy harp', Irish Independent 03, p.15.1985.

(4) 'Scuffles at Coursing protest', Irish Independent, Feb.06, p.10,1986.

(5) 'Coursing field sabotaged, farmer loses damages claim', Kilkenny People, May 9, p.4,1986.

(6) 'Threat to sabotage coursing, Evening Press, Dublin, June 6, p.3

(7) John Kilraine,'Born to be wild', Evening Herald, Dublin, sept. 8, p.17,1986.

(8) 'Glass on farmers field', Irish Press, Dublin, Sept,12, p.3,1986.

(9) 'Blood sports group condemn attack', Irish Press, Dublin, Oct.23, p.5,1986.

(10) 'Anti-blood sports group flee mob', Irish Independent, Dublin, Oct. 28, p.10,1986.

(11) Derek Cunningham, 'Gardai probe transfer of coursing meet', the Kerryman, Nov. 14, p.13,1986.

(12) 'Threat to coursing', the Kerryman, Dec. 26, p.1,1986.

(13) ALF SG Diary of Actions, 'actions from abroad', Oct. 86, #1, p.4,1986. (UK)

1987

(1) Tony Purcell, 'Protest over Coursing', Evening Echo, Cork, Jan.7, p.1,1987.

(2) Maureen fox, 'Animal Liberation Masquerades as Cowardice', Irish Examiner, Cork, Jan.12, p.3,1987.

(3) 'Anti-blood sports groups linked claim', Evening Echo, Jan.22, p.3,1987.

(4) "ALF Arson in Dublin', Irish Examiner, Jan.23, p.20,1987.

(5) Tom Reddy, 'Mink farm target of letter bomb', Irish Independent, Jan.23, p.1,1987.

(6) 'Attack puts coursing club on 24-hr alert', Irish Examiner, Cork, Jan 8, p.4,1987.

(7) 'Animal rights protest', Irish Press, Jan.24, p.3,1987.

(8) Ray O'Hanlon, 'Bomb hoaxes "put jobs in jeopardy" ', Irish Press, Dublin, Jan.31, p.3,1987.

(9) 'Animal Front responsible', Irish Press, Feb.12, p.2,1987.

(10) ALF SG Diary of Actions, April #1, p.4,1987. (UK)

(11) Tom Lavery, 'Animal Front link in hay blaze case', Irish Press, Dublin, Feb.17, p.3,1987.

(12) Tacks 'spread on land" ', Evening Echo, Cork, Feb.24, p. 5,1987.

(13) 'Arson attack claimed', Irish Independent, March 30, p.9,198

(14) ALF Supporters Group, 'actions from abroad', March, p.4,1987. (UK)

(15)'Protest at Garda station "Rubbish" ', The Nationalist (Tipp.), Apr.11, p.3,1987.

(16) 'Animal Group claims Bombs', Irish Press, May 20, p.4,1987

(17) Isabel Conway, 'Kenny show attacked', Irish Press, June 5, p.7,1987.

(18) 'Spate of attacks on butchers' shops', Irish Press, Dublin, June 2, p.5,1987; ALF SG, 'Diary of Actions, International actions, March #2, 1987.

(19) 'Gardai probe shampoos "hoax"', Evening Echo, Cork, July27, p.2,1987.

(20) ALF Supporters Group Diary of Actions, 'International Actions'. 4,Nov, #3, 1987. (UK)

(21) ALF Supporters Group, Diary of Actions, 'International Actions', p.4, Nov. #3,1987. (UK)

(22) Dan Collins, 'Fire gang hit wrong farm', Evening Echo, Cork, Oct.2, p.1,1987.

(23) 'Animal Front link to attack on shop', Irish Independent, Dublin, Oct.15, p.11,1987

(24) 'Challenge to animal libbers', Irish Examiner, Cork, Oct.6, p.8,1987.

(25) '"Rights" group set fire to factory', Belfast Telegraph, Oct.7, p.27,1987.

(26) 'Letter threat to farmers', Irish Independent, Dublin, Nov.5, p9,1987.

(27) ' False info' Evening Echo (Cork) Oct.20, p.6,1987.

1988

(1) 'Anti-blood sports man wrote threatening letter Court told', Irish Examiner, Cork, Jan.29, p.26,1988.

(2) 'Charges withdrawn by State in Coursing case, Munster Express, Feb.5, p.7,1988

(3) Eugene Molloney,'Animal group admits attack', Evening Herald, Dublin, April 4, p.4,1988.

(4) Tom Casey, 'Coursing: Cllr hits out after threats', Evening Echo, Cork, June17, p.18,1988.

(5) 'Tacks scare in Lib war on coursing', Irish Press, Dublin.Sept.20, p.2,1988.

(6) John Murphy, 'Master McGrath back to his best', Irish Examiner, Cork, June 1, p.20,1988.

1989

(1) 'Fair organiser tells of hate campaign', Belfast Telegraph, March 14, p.27,1989.

(2) 'Two on arson charge', Belfast Telegraph, March 25, p.20,1989.

(3) 'Bomb alert closes McDonalds', Evening Herald, Dublin, June 24, p.2,1989.

(4) Des Mullan, 'Coursing: officials warned', Evening Herald, Dublin, August 21, p.1,1989.

(5) 'Animal rights group threat criticised', Evening Echo, Cork, Aug.22, p1,1989.

(6) John Martin, 'Anti-coursing body must speak out', Irish Independent, Dublin, Aug.22, p.14,1989.

(7) 'Animal lib Coursing bomb threat', Irish Press, Dublin, Sept.26, p.3,1989.

(8) 'Anti-blood sports activist acquitted of arson threats', Kilkenny People, Nov.10, p.1,1989.

(9) ' Vandals liked to Coursing disruption", Enniscorthy Guardian, Nov. 16, 1989.

(10) Janet Devlin, 'Shampoo cleared from shelves after animal lib threat', Belfast Telegraph, Dec.20, p.38,1989.

(11) 'Anti-fur attacks on shops', Irish Press, Dublin, Dec.30, p.14,1989.

1990

(1) 'Group News' HOWL#44, p.2, Summer 1990

(2) 'Shops warned to check cosmetics', Irish Examiner, Cork, April 14, p.1,1990.

(3) 'ALF issue warning after attack on club', Belfast Telegraph, May 21, p.3,1990.

(4) Gwyneth Jones, 'Fair organisers lash animal lib vandalism', Belfast Telegraph, July 2, p.26,1990.

(5) 'Track blaze "a start"', Irish Independent, Dublin, Sept. 3, p.5,1990

(6) Brian McLaughlin, 'Animal group to" bomb dog courses" ', Irish Press, Dublin, Sept. 13, p.12,1990.

(7) 'Poison threat to water supplies', The Kerryman, Sept. 28, p.1,1990.

(8) 'Water taste fears', Irish Examiner, Oct.15, p.5,1990.

(9) Dan Collins, 'Forensics probe restaurant bomb', Evening Echo, Cork, Oct. 29, p.2,1990.

(10) Tom Brady, 'Gardai in animal lib gang bust', Evening Herald, Dublin, Nov. 20, p.1,1990.

(11) 'Anti blood sports drive', Belfast Telegraph, Nov.13, p.12,1990.

(12) 'Bomb scare hoax at Killarney hotel' The Kerryman, Nov.1990

(13) 'Poisoned turkeys' threat', Irish Examiner, Dec. 18,1990.

(14) 'Slogans daubed on door', Belfast Telegraph, Dec.24, p.6,1990.

1991

(1) 'We attacked shops, say rights group', Belfast Telegraph, Jan.14, p.32,1991.

(2) 'Hunt hit by saboteurs, Belfast Telegraph, Feb.27, p.35,1991.

(3) 'Shops hit by animal protesters', Belfast Telegraph, Feb.11, p.30,1991.

(4) Linda Brien, 'Activists claim farm arson', Belfast Telegraph, March 11, p.25,1991.

(5) 'Animal activists admit damage', Belfast Telegraph, March 29, p.51,1991.

(6) 'ALF claims farm attack', Belfast Telegraph, April 20, p.13,1991.

(7) 'Attack on kennels claimed', Belfast Telegraph, July 15, p.27,1991.

(8) 'Warning from animal activists', Belfast Telegraph, July 20, p.2,1991.

(9) 'Major arms cache dug up in North', Irish Independent, July 29, p.3,1991

(10) 'Animal liberation Front", Belfast Telegraph, July 22, p.32,1991.

(11) 'Animal libbers grab hens', Belfast Telegraph, July 30, p.7,1991.

(12),'ALF claim attack, Belfast Telegraph, Aug.2, p.3,1991.

(13) 'Bomb found', Evening Herald, Aug.6, p.47,1991.

(14) ' ALF ban demanded', Irish Examiner, Aug.27, p.22,1991.

(15) 'Arson attack', Belfast Telegraph, Sept.13, p 2. ,1991.

(16) 'Call to ban ALF rejected by Minister', Belfast Telegraph, Oct.18, p.49,1991.

(17) Neil Derbyshire, 'Lucozade withdrawn in UK poison scare', Irish Independent, Nov.14, p.12,1991.

(18) 'Woman claims injury after hunt scuffle', Belfast Telegraph, Nov.19, p.6,1991.

1992

(1) Support Animal Rights Prisoners (SARP), Newsletter Jan., p.14,1992. (UK)

(2) SARP Newsletter Nov. 1992, p. 12. (UK)

(3) 'Front attack on meat shops?', Evening Herald, Dublin, June 11, p.99,1991.

1993

(1) John Murphy, "Activists attacked', Irish Examiner (Cork), Oct. 11, p. 3, 1993

(2) Dan Collins, " Anti-blood sports man is attacked", Irish Examiner, Nov.11, p.5,1993

(3) Darwin Templeton, 'Burger chain faces threats', Belfast Telegraph, Dec.26, p.3,1991.

(4) Lindy McDowell, 'Chasing the hunt', Belfast Telegraph, Dec.29, p.10,1993.

1994

(1) 'New violent anti-coursing campaign bid', Evening Echo, Cork, Jan.13, p .33,1994.

(2) Darwin Templeton, 'Legal move by saboteur after clash with huntsman', Belfast Telegraph, Jan.18, p.5,1991.

(3) Darwin Templeton, 'Police probe bomb threats', Belfast Telegraph, Feb.26, p.1,1994.

(4) Ralph Riegal,'Animal terrorists target Munster', Irish Examiner, Cork, March 7, p. 1,1994.

(5) ' "We started fire "animal front', Sunday Independent, Dublin, May 22, p.1,1994.

(6) 'ALF attack pensioners home by mistake', Belfast Telegraph, July 30, p.1,1994.

(7) Darwin Templeton, 'Animal rights borders breached', Belfast Telegraph, Mar. 5, p.3,1994.

(8)

(9) Darwin Templeton, 'Animal rights woman cleared', Belfast Telegraph, Aug.26, p.39,1994.

(10) Ralph Reigal, 'Video parcel bomb blushes', Irish Examiner, Cork, Oct. 5, p.11,1994.

(11) letter to the editor, Galway Advertiser, Nov.? p .?1994

1995

(1) 'A blazing row', Galway Advertiser, Jan. 1, p.1,1995

(2) 'Animal rights extremist firebombs?', Irish Press, Dublin, Jan.16, p .6,1995.

(3) 'Sabotage sparks blood sports row', Irish Independent, Dublin, Feb.6, p.16,1995.

(4) 'Extremist 'hoaxers'', Belfast Telegraph, July 5, p.26,1995.

(5) 'Group News', HOWL# 60, p.5, Winter 1995/96.

1996

(1) Ralph Riegal,'Port security intensified after tip off', Irish Examiner, Cork, March 20, p .6,1996.

(2) 'Save our Stags', HOWL# 62, p. 10, Autumn 1996.

(3) Ralph Reigal,'UK militants threaten to bomb Irish sea ports used for live cattle exports', Irish Examiner, Cork, Aug.24, p.1,1996.

(4) Ralph Reigal,'Arson threat to cattle exports', Irish Examiner, Cork, Aug.29, p.32,1996.

(5) Ralph Reigal,'Travellers expected as ALF warn of ports attack', Irish Examiner, Cork, Aug.28, p.6,1996.

(6) 'Fiery revenge of an unhappy hooker', Sunday Independent, Dublin, Sept.8, p.3,1996.

(7) 'Gardai get details of ALF militants', Irish Examiner, Cork, Sept.9, p.28,1996.

1997

(1) Michael Quinn,'Tally-ho as whips lash out at fox hunt', Irish Independent, Dublin, Jan. 27, p.4,1997.

(2) 'Hunt saboteur failed to appear in court', Munster Express, Feb.14, p.32,1997.

(3) https://www.wildlifeguardian.co.uk/hunting/hunt-convictions/ ; https://network23.org/northwaleshuntsabs/2020/03/11/the-struggling-flint-and-denbigh-hunt/

(4) 'British anti-blood sports activists disrupt Waterford Hunt', Munster Express, Jan.31, p.17,1997.

(5) 'Hunt upheaval', Kilkenny People, March 14, p.1,1997.

(6) Brian Winders, 'Cruel Practices" on pig farm are filmed', Irish Examiner, Cork, April 11, p.39,1996.

(7) Irish Examiner, Cork, Aug.14, p.10,1997.

1998

(1) Greg Harkin, 'Loyalists try to kill man with keep-fit video', Irish Examiner, Feb.20, p.4,1998.

1999

(1) 'Angry huntsmen abandon fox to chase saboteurs', Irish Independent, Feb.22, p.3,1999.

2000

(1) Conor Keane, 'Animal Liberation Front expected to strike again', Irish Examiner, Cork, Oct.25, p.6,2000.

2001

(1) Conor Keane,'6,000 coursing fans disappointed as unidentified saboteurs steal hares', Irish Examiner, Cork, Jan.3, p.34,2001.

(2) 'Gardai called to hunt protest', Irish Independent, Dublin, Jan.15, p.9,2001.

(3) 'Animal rights activists slated', Alan Jacque, Limerick Leader, Dec.5, p.1,2001.

2002

(1)

2003

(1) 'Scuffles at traditional St. Stephan's day hunt', John Feeney, Meath Chronicle, Jan.4, p.3,2003.

(2) http://directaction.info/news_feb19_03.htm

(3) http://directaction.info/news_june02_03.htm

(4) http://directaction.info/news_june20_03.htm

(5) Carol Duffy, 'Air horn hunt saboteur jailed for two months', Irish Examiner, June 20, p.6,2003.

(6) http://directaction.info/news_july22_03.htm

2004

(1) http://directaction.info/news_jan11a_04.htm

(2) 'Hunt scuffles', Meath Chronicle, Jan.3, p.18,2004.

(3) "AIB pulls it support for Ward Union hunt', Meath Chronicle, April 3, p.39.2004.

(4) http://directaction.info/news_june13_04.htm

(5) Irish Independent, " Clash at circus over animal rights", July 8, p.10,2004.

(6) http://directaction.info/news_oct05a_04.htm

(7) http://directaction.info/news_oct16_04.htm

(8) http://directaction.info/news_nov12_04.htm

(9) http://directaction.info/news_nov12a_04.htm

(10) http://directaction.info/news_dec08_04.htm

(11) http://directaction.info/news_dec08_04.htm

(12) http://directaction.info/news_dec07a_04.htm

2005

(1)

(2) http://directaction.info/news_jan09a_05.htm

'Hare coursing venue attacked', ALF SG Ireland, Jan 9th, 2005.

(3) http://directaction.info/news_feb20_05.htm

(4) http://directaction.info/news_may11_05.htm

(5)

(6) http://directaction.info/news_may31_05.htm

(7) http://directaction.info/news_june02_05.htm

(8)

(9) http://directaction.info/news_july22_05.htm

(10) http://directaction.info/news_aug11a_05.htm

(11) http://directaction.info/news_aug14_05.htm

(12) http://directaction.info/news_oct18_05.htm

(13) http://directaction.info/news_oct26_05.htm

(14) http://directaction.info/news_dec04b_05.htm

(15)

(16) http://directaction.info/news_dec24_05.htm

(17)

2006

(1) http://directaction.info/news_jan01_06.htm
(2) http://directaction.info/news_mar29_06.htm
(3) http://directaction.info/news_apr12b_06.htm
(4) http://directaction.info/news_may13_06.htm
(5) http://directaction.info/news_june18_06.htm
(6) http://directaction.info/news_aug03b_06.htm
(7) http://directaction.info/mag_8.htm
(8) http://directaction.info/news_oct09b_06.htm
(9) http://directaction.info/news_oct09b_06.htm
(10) http://directaction.info/news_nov05b_06.htm
(11) http://directaction.info/news_dec15c_06.htm
(12) http://directaction.info/news_dec26_06.htm

2007

(1) http://www.directaction.info/news_jan04b_07.htm
(2) http://www.directaction.info/news_jan29_07.htm
(3) http://www.directaction.info/news_mar01_07.htm
(4) http://www.directaction.info/news_mar01_07.htm
(5) http://www.directaction.info/news_mar01_07.htm
(6) http://www.directaction.info/news_mar01_07.htm
(7) http://www.directaction.info/news_mar12b_07.htm
(8) http://www.directaction.info/news_mar16b_07.htm
(9) http://www.directaction.info/news_mar30_07.htm
(10) http://www.directaction.info/news_apr28c_07.htm
(11) http://www.directaction.info/news_may14_07.htm ;
(12) http://www.directaction.info/news_may14_07.htm
(13) http://www.directaction.info/news_jun12b_07.htm
(14) http://www.directaction.info/news_july26_07.htm
(15) http://www.directaction.info/news_aug02_07.htm ; http://www.directaction.info/news_sep07_07.htm
(16) http://www.directaction.info/news_sep19_07.htm
(17) http://www.directaction.info/news_oct12_07.htm

2008

(1) http://directaction.info/news_jan02b_08.htm
(2) http://directaction.info/news_jan02b_08.htm
(3) http://directaction.info/news_mar22_08.htm

(4) http://directaction.info/news_may04c_08.htm

(5) http://directaction.info/news_jun07c_08.htm

(6) http://directaction.info/news_oct18_08.htm

2009

(1)

(2) http://directaction.info/news_july14_09.htm; http://directaction.info/news_july16_09.htm

(3) http://directaction.info/news_aug10_09.htm

(4) http://directaction.info/news_sep30_09.htm

(5) http://directaction.info/news_oct12b_09.htm

(6) http://directaction.info/news_oct18_09.htm

(7) http://directaction.info/news_dec11_09.htm

(8) Andrew Phelan ' Fur shop owner hit activist and called her a Nazi' Evening Herald (Dublin) Oct.8, p. 17, 2011

2010

(1) http://directaction.info/news_jan18_10.htm

(2) http://directaction.info/news_feb25_10.htm

(3) http://directaction.info/news_mar24_10.htm

(4) http://directaction.info/news_july18b_10.htm

(5) http://directaction.info/news_aug09_10.htm

(6) http://directaction.info/news_sep05_10.htm

(7) http://directaction.info/news_sep18_10.htm

(8) http://directaction.info/news_sep15_10.htm

(9) http://directaction.info/news_sep29_10.htm

(10) http://directaction.info/news_oct26b_10.htm

2011

(1) http://directaction.info/news_mar31b_11.htm

(2) 'Animal rights protester alleged she was assaulted', Connaught Telegraph, Nov. 29, p.7, 2011

(3) http://directaction.info/news_apr14b_11.htm ; http://directaction.info/news_apr18_11.htm

(4) Conor Feehan, 'Animal rights activist jailed over KFC attack', Evening Herald, Dublin, p. April 2011

2012

(1) http://directaction.info/news_jan03_12.htm
(2) http://directaction.info/news_mar24_12.htm

2013

(1) http://directaction.info/news_may21b_13.htm
(2) http://directaction.info/news_oct10_13.htm ; http://directaction.info/news_oct13_13.htm ; http://directaction.info/news_oct29_13.htm

2014

(1)
(2) http://directaction.info/news_june24b_14.htm
(3) http://directaction.info/news_oct14_14.htm
(4) http://directaction.info/news_oct29_14.htm
(5) http://directaction.info/news_nov02_14.htm
(6) http://directaction.info/news_dec26_14.htm

2015

(1) http://directaction.info/news_may13_15.htm

2016

(1) http://directaction.info/news_jan16_16.htm
(2) http://directaction.info/news_mar15b_16.htm

2017

0

2018

(1) - 'Group calls for closure of mink farm' Donegal News, March 2, p.34, 2018.

2019

(1) Mark Hilliard, 'Pig farm protest to prompt meeting of Gardai and Agriculturalists', Irish Times, June 3,2019 ; https://www.irishtimes.com/news/social-affairs/pig-farm-

protest-to-prompt-meeting-of-garda%C3%AD-and-agriculturalists-1.3944463

(2) http://directaction.info/news_apr17_19.htm

2020

(1) Rachel O'Connor, 'Vegan activists "liberate" a pig from farm in Ballymena', Irish Post,Jan.15,2020 ; https://www.irishpost.com/news/warning-graphic-images-vegan-activists-liberate-pig-farm-ballymena-177285

(2)   https://unoffensiveanimal.is/2020/06/26/7-individuals-aided-in-their-escape-from-a-facility/

(3)'Down farmers raise concerns over hunting with dogs", https://www.farminglife.com/country-and-farming/down-farmers-raise-concerns-over-hunting-dogs-1741423

(4)   https://unoffensiveanimal.is/2020/07/03/thirty-five-ducks-rescued-from-a-shoot-infrastructure-destroyed/

2021

(1)   https://unoffensiveanimal.is/2021/06/26/magpies-liberated-from-larsen-trap-in-ireland/

(2)   https://unoffensiveanimal.is/2021/09/26/three-hunting-towers-destroyed-in-ireland/

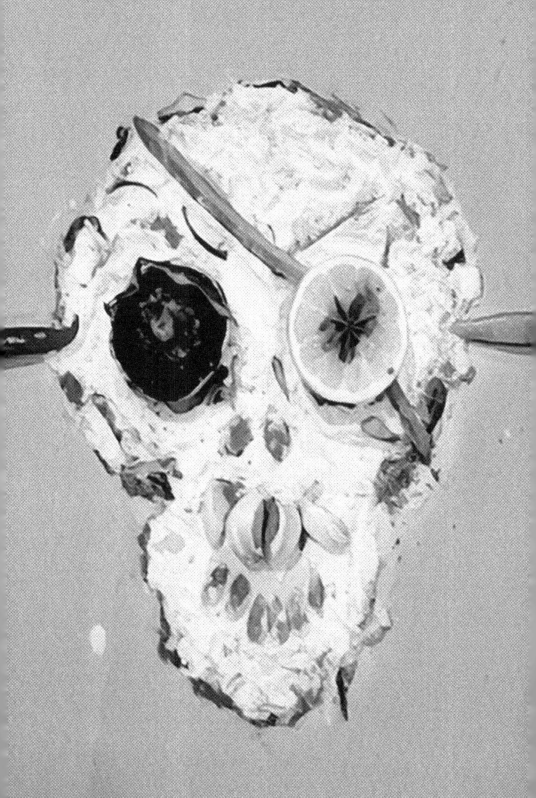

CHAPTER FIVE - US AND THEM - A SABOTEURS STORY

"Sport Hunting is a sickness, a perversion and a danger and should be recognised as such. People who get their 'amusement' from hunting and killing other defenceless animals can only be suffering from a mental disorder. In a world with boundless opportunities for amusement, it's detestable that anyone would choose to get thrills from killing others who ask for nothing from life but the chance to remain alive."
Roger Moore AKA James Bond 007

Hunt Sabotage began sporadic life in Ireland in mid-1980's but has existed formally in Great Britain since 1963 when a young journalist named John Prestidge witnessed a heavily pregnant deer being chased down by the local Stag Hunt. Both the deer and her foetus were torn to pieces by dogs in the middle of a village in Devon as the Hunt cheered and jeered. Incensed by this deranged and feral violence, Prestidge formed the first Hunt Saboteurs group. The idea was to actively disrupt the hunting of foxes and deer by distracting the hounds with horn calls and food. Chunks of meat would be thrown to the hungry hounds causing absolute chaos and making it impossible to organise them into a coherent pack. Tactics have since evolved, and meat is no longer used.

This wasn't the first-time people had disrupted blood sports in Britain, however.

Anecdotal evidence exists– in the form of letters written into HOWL- that tell of RAF crew in World War 2 laying false trails of aniseed balls to disrupt the local Hunt, who were widely resented for being rich toffs. This is impossible to confirm though.

In 1958 members of the League Against Cruel Sports (LACS) experimented in sabotage by laying down chemical scents in long meandering lines to distract and mislead the hounds of the Devon and Somerset Staghounds. The experiment was a success and was repeated in 1962.

Also in 1962, Gwen Barter, another LACS activist, sat on the bonnet of the lead vehicle of the Norwich Staghounds Hunt and refused to move, Rosa Parks-style. She stayed there, holding a placard, until the Hunt simply gave up and went home. Gwen repeated the tactic 8 months later by sitting on top of a burrow that a fox had 'gone to ground' in during a foxhunt. Again, the Hunt backed off and went away, unsure of how to respond and no doubt hoping this sort of thing didn't catch on....

*above - How it all began, the Rosa Parks of the modern animal rights movement **Gwen Barter** obstructing the Norwich Staghounds Hunt, March 1962. This is the first known act of civil disobedience to protect non-human animals. Gwen sat on the front of the leading hunt convoy vehicle of the Norwich Stag hounds hunt and refused to move. The Hunt simply gave up and went home. She repeated the act later in the year. Gwen was an inspiration to the embryonic Hunt Sabotage movement beginning a few years later. Her sign reads "**The cruel, barbaric ritual of carted deer hunting must stop now.**"*

Image from 'Sabotage- the story of the Hunt Saboteurs Association.

When John Prestidge formed the first Hunt Saboteurs Association in Devon in December 1963, he took inspiration from the effective tactics of recent LACS activists. False scent trails, horn and voice calls mimicking the hunters, smoke canisters, flares, food, anything to distract and disorient the Hunt and hounds was tried and tested.

The phenomenon spread quickly, and new groups sprang up around Britain over the next few years. Initially caught off guard, the hunting community's reaction was as predictable as it was aggressive. Hunters and Hunt Sabotage soon became bywords for violence and have remained so to this day. The landed gentry and their fanbase do not like being answered back to and will use all the considerable power and violence at their disposal to keep the great unwashed out of their way.

In a sense, hunt sabotage as a sustained, widespread movement should not exist. If you have ever tried to rally people behind a cause you will know how difficult it can be. Even a cause that will directly benefit them, like a demand for better pay or conditions at work, can prove impossible.

Consider this with Hunt Sabotage.

Every Saboteur is subject to early morning starts, long days, atrocious weather, endless threats of and actual violence, hostile police and media, walking and running for miles across boggy fields, trying to read maps and blow hunting horns and, despite the rumours, no free packed lunch courtesy of the League Against Cruel Sports, Socialist Workers Party or Greenpeace.

All to protect a wild animal you barely ever see, even when out sabbing.

How many recruits do you think will flock to that cause?

Plenty as it turns out.

above-hunt sabs of 1964 - **John Prestige,** founder of the Hunt Saboteurs Association, on the far right. *Image from 'Sabotage- the story of the Hunt Saboteurs Association.*

The movement flourished almost immediately, with public support being voiced by such varied celebrities as xenophobic Tory astronomer Sir Patrick Moore and three members of beat-pop group Herman's Hermits (!)

Facing down the inevitable violent reaction and often biased policing, the HSA grew throughout the 1970's. A BBC documentary on the group aired in 1975 and attracted a surge in support and membership. The maturation of the emerging Punk rock movement was another pivotal point in the movement's evolution. Lots of Punks were sympathetic to the anti-hunting cause and were happy to spend a day in the countryside sowing some benign anarchy.

Hunt Sabotage in Britain grew massively throughout the 1980's and 90's, as did tactics and experience. Out went chaotic tactics like throwing smoke bombs and chunks of meat about, in came *gizmos*, citronella spray and hunting horns. Sab groups all over Great Britain became increasingly professional and effective. Better communications and recording devices, increased understanding of how hunts work and how best to sab them, effective counter-reactions to violence from hunt thugs, detailed understanding of the law, all combined to create an unstoppable momentum.

All blood sports were condemned and targeted, including Fishing and even Falconry, despite the inevitable backlash in the media. The HSA maintained a cohesive and consistent line of clear thinking when every other animal rights/welfare group was bowing to perceived majority opinion, terrified of losing support and income.

Some sab groups became notoriously aggressive in response to the violence they encountered and would turn up at hunts in a convoy of battered transit vans with metal grills over the windscreen, all wearing black with balaclavas on. The South London 'Brixton Mob' were the 'go-to' group when you needed your local hunt sorted out. Their mere presence was frequently enough to send the hunt packing before they even got started. If the Hunt were foolhardy enough to go out, the Brixton response was to overwhelm them with numbers and hostility, quantity being a quality in itself. The anarcho-punk scene was in full swing at this time and became a fertile recruiting ground for the hunt saboteur movement.

Violent encounters between saboteurs and the Hunt and their supporters was a weekly event at this time. Thousands were injured, hundreds arrested and three people killed during this twenty-year period.

JOCKS IN A BOX – above – *Fred 'Nosher' Powell (far left giving the evils) and his merry hard men arriving at a Surrey Union Hunt to teach the Sabs a lesson, 1992. Following the Unions defeat at the Battle of Holmbury Hill, they drafted in a bunch of East End villains and thugs led by bit-actor and all-round tough geezer wot gets things done innit Nosher Powell, extra/stuntman for dozens of shit movies including Eat the Rich, which also features Lemmy. After a whole day of fighting these guys met their match on a narrow foot bridge where they ended up surrounded and battered into submission, reminiscent of the Battle of Cannae in 216 BC. Nosher and Chums surrendered to the mob of saboteurs, and they crawled back to the East End, never to be seen or heard from again. source HSA archive.*

above – **the Brixton posse** – *for when the going gets tough. By no means was every Saboteur a black-clad tough-nut but the historical record shows, to my mind at least, that without a sustained and assertive response to violence from the Hunting fraternity, the movement would not have survived beyond the 1970's. source HSA archive.*

Relentless violence against unarmed, peaceful saboteurs was commonplace. Two Saboteurs – Tom Worby and Mike Hill – were killed while sabbing in the early 1990's. Tom, aged just 15, was hit by a vehicle being driven by Hunter Tony Ball in Cambridge in 1993 and dragged to his death. Two years earlier, Mike Hill, aged 18, was out sabbing the Cheshire Beagles. Along with two colleagues, he sat atop the stationary hounds' van to prevent it from moving. The driver, huntsman Allan Summersgill, started up and moved off anyway, speeding up as he went. The three sabs, clinging on to the roof as Summersgill swerved and sped along narrow country lanes. They were banging on the roof and windows begging him to stop but Summersgill ignored them and increased his speed. The three decided to jump for it when the vehicle slowed down to take a corner, but Mike misjudged his jump and landed between the car and the trailer, crushing him instantly.

Neither huntsman was ever charged or convicted of any crime. Summersgill went into hiding afterwards and his (empty) house was burned to the ground by the ALF a week after Mike's death.

One confrontation involving particularly large numbers on both sides became known as the Battle of Holmbury Hill. In January 1991, the Surrey Union Foxhunt had ambushed local saboteurs, sending five of them to the hospital with broken wrists, noses and fractured skulls.

Behaviour like this must be challenged – justice must be done and must be *seen to be* done.

COME AND HAVE A GO…. *if you think you're hard enough. Employees of* **Countrywatch** *provide 'security' at the Surrey Union hunt, 1993. Led by New Zealand born David Dunn, an ex-soldier, this private security firm specialised in attacking saboteurs with bats and staves. Their violence, facilitated by the Police, led to regular "national hits' by Saboteurs on the hunts that employed them, culminating in the* **Battle of Stagden Cross** *on January 23rd 1993,when, once again, hundreds of saboteurs took on and defeated the 'might' of this State-approved thuggeratti. The violence that day started when Countrywatch goons began pushing Sabs off public footpaths with threats of extreme violence. This blatant illegality became the catalyst for the assembled Saboteurs to fight back and a huge scrap erupted between two hundred Sabs armed with hunting horns and citronella spray versus one hundred Security with their staves and iron bars and Alsatian dogs spilling into the fields on either side of a bridlepath. source HSA archive.*

The following Saturday, *three hundred* saboteurs from across the Southeast turned up to show their support for their comrades. The Hunt met at a pub in Forest Green and only the local sabs went there, everyone else stayed hidden in woods that surrounded the village. As the Hunt finished their sherry's and galloped off with hounds in tow, hundreds of Saboteurs began to mob up ahead of them, still hidden in the trees. As the unsuspecting hunters rode into an elevated copse called Holmbury Hill, they were rushed from three sides by three hundred masked up sabs.

Countrywatch Security and the hunts supporters were once again overwhelmed by the righteous anger and violence from the saboteurs. They and the Hunt were beaten back into a small farmyard where they stayed, badly bruised and bloodied, effectively surrendering the ground to the saboteurs. Like the unpaid thugs who came before them, Countrywatch could give it, but- and this is crucial - they couldn't take it. Five policemen were also injured.

above -**Countrywatch Security** *illegally blocking public footpaths for the Surrey Union Foxhunt, 1993. This highly provocative behaviour provoked the disturbance which followed immediately after this photo was taken. Image used with permission from Mike Huskisson.*

The leading riders were dragged off their horses and set upon, dozens of hunt supporters were swarmed by saboteurs and shown Heavy Manners. Over the next few hours, the Hunt were beaten and battered all over the woods as they tried fighting back then turned and fled. Though they had similar numbers out that day, they were taken completely by surprise and the "Anti's" had a stunning victory.

Veteran Saboteur Colin Skilton recalls the effect this confrontation had on the Surrey Union Hunt – "They didn't meet again on a Saturday for *ten years* and never launched any large-scale attacks on sabs. The number of riders also dropped dramatically causing the hunt to almost fold through lack of support and money."

'Security' firms dropped out of favour following this beating, and not just with the Hunts. Police initially welcomed their presence as it meant the 'Stewards' could do the dirty work of physically confronting and ejecting Sabs from privately owned land while the overpaid and overfed constabulary could stand back and watch out for any breaches of 'reasonable force', all on triple time of course. This didn't pan out like they hoped.

The March 1993 edition of 'The Law', Essex Police forces internal monthly magazine, devotes two whole pages to the Battle of Stagden Cross. The Forces Liaison Officer for Hunting, Superintendent Bob Good said of Security firms (they call them 'Stewards'- more bucolic) protecting hunts in general "The initial thoughts were that we would be able to reduce our manpower if Stewards were successful. In the event that has not proved possible, and I don't think it will be possible for the future." Local Huntsman for the Essex foxhounds Paul Dixey added smugly "We think the Police acted extremely well and we are greatly indebted to them, particularly for the amazing performance they put up at the Battle of Stagden Cross when 30 of them kept a cordon protecting us from the protesters". As long as you're OK, Paul. That's all that matters, eh?

above – *issue # 4 of the **Class War** newspaper, 1984, subtle as ever. Class War regularly cited the hunt sabs and the ALF as sources of inspiration. At the movement's height in the mid-1980's, their rabble-rousing tabloid sold many thousands each issue and was characterised by an enthusiastic endorsement of violence against the rich, police and fascists.*

Insurrectionary Anarchists were drawn to hunt sabotage not least because it provided an opportunity to have an organised go at the social elite. Unlike toppling the State, sabotaging a foxhunt was an achievable goal and pissed off the Rich no end. Plus, a fox gets to live another day and it's a chance to get out in the countryside. What's not to like?

Indeed, the new-wave anarchist Left were the only ones who seemed genuinely interested in the animal rights movement at this time. Most other left-wing groups and individuals regarded animal rights as a distraction at best, a betrayal of the working class at worst, an attitude that's barely changed since. Which is ironic because throughout the 1980's and 90's, the animal rights movement posed a far more potent threat to the Establishment than all the radical Left combined. And then some. stock image.

THE HUMAN LEAGUE - above- *Marx and Engels scoffing at the hopeless bourgeois sentimentality in an early issue of 'The Vegetarian Messenger', newsletter of the recently formed UK Vegetarian Society. Painting by E. Capiro, circa 1848/49.*

"From Each according to his Species, to each according to his Humanity"- Karl Marx , author of the Communist Humanifesto.
Two legs good, four legs food.

*Both Karl Marx and BFF Friedrich Engels deserve commendation for their analysis of the historical epochs that developed thus far into Capitalism, and their concerns for poor and oppressed people everywhere. If only they had taken a few more steps back to see the bigger picture that includes our non-human animal cousins and, of course, the ultimate Superstructure that everything else depends on – Earth/Nature/Gaia/ the Biosphere. To witness a modern-day **revolutionary Marxist-Leninist** magically transform into a histrionic **Reactionary Conservative**, simply talk favourably about animal rights. If all a 'successful' Class Struggle does is exchange one set of animal oppressors with another, then it's just as unsustainable and cruel (maybe even more so) as its predecessor and therefore not worth getting out of bed for. Thankfully there is a new wave of Marxist philosophers who have taken on board the need to develop their approach in light of contemporary concerns including environmental, animal and feminist issues, Corey Lee Wrenn (author of the other book on animal rights in Ireland, 'Animals in Irish Society') and Black Power icon Angela Davis amongst them. stock image.*

BRAVE HEART V Army of Cartmans - *Irish Kev* *stands up to the entire Surrey Union "Security Team" of **Cartman** look-a-likes, circa 1990 – these thugs were sent packing at the legendary **Battle of Holmbury Hill** in January 1991. A 'National Hit' organised in retaliation for five saboteurs hospitalised the week before saw 300 saboteurs descend on the Hunt, their Security and their Support. A pitched battle erupted with the saboteurs overwhelming the Opposition with numbers and aggression. Police made dozens of arrests, but all charges were later dropped. It is testament to the effectiveness of the hunt sabotage movement that the Hunting fraternity felt the need to employ extra security on top of the free State security provided only too willingly by the Police. Even then they failed. Source HSA archive.*

Hunting with dogs was banned by the UK Parliament in 2004 but remains legal in Northern Ireland as well as the Republic. This position was reinforced at a vote in December 2021 when the Northern Ireland Assembly at Stormont voted 45-38 to continue to allow hunting with dogs. Disgracefully, the so-called party of working-class republicanism - Sinn Fin - voted as a unified block *in favour* of continuing to allow hunting with dogs, a 'sport' invented and sustained by the Protestant Ascendency they apparently stand so firmly against. Tiocfaidh ar La and Tally Ho Old Chap!

For shame.

When the hunting fraternity hired thugs to beat up sabs, some Saboteurs met fire with fire. Informal offshoots of the HSA like the Hunt Retribution Squad (HRS) emerged to tackle the problematic hunts head on. HRS activists typically acted covertly in small groups, damaging property, and posting threatening letters and bombs to Hunters.

On occasion, however, they appeared *en masse* to ambush hunters in the field.

One notorious example of this occurred at the Hursley Hambledon Foxhut in Bishops Waltham, Hampshire in December 1997. One hundred HRS activists descended on the Hunt as it was in full swing and for ten minutes smashed every vehicle in sight with bats and iron bars. Hunt supporters who tried to intervene were attacked, three were hospitalised.

Police arrested 42 activists as they fled the scene, but all charges were later dropped due to lack of evidence.

Violence against Saboteurs from the Hunt decreased significantly following the attack.

TOUGH ON ANIMAL ABUSE AND TOUGH ON THE CAUSES OF ANIMAL ABUSE - above
– *The **Brixton Mob** in action – pointing, shouting, scuffling, trespassing, brawling, their mere presence was usually enough to send the Hunt packing or prevent them even leaving their kennels. Police often spent thousands protecting Hunts on a given Saturday, all of it from the taxpayer's purse. Unlike with other 'sporting' events that require an often very heavy police presence, like football, the Hunting clubs were never asked to chip in for the costs of their police guard. source HSA archive.*

In truth, the Hunting fraternity essentially already had their own private security firm – the Police - before they resorted to hiring extra muscle. They even had their own Parliament, at least in the UK, where the House of Lords was (and still is) filled with unelected blood-sport enthusiasts who get paid $300 a day (at least) to negate democracy at will. They shot down every Bill ever proposed against blood sports by the House of Commons for a century until the rarely invoked Parliament Act of 1911 was used to break their stranglehold on democracy in 2003. The Police were often at the command of the Master of Foxhounds just as surely as the hounds were. In short, if you wish to witness just how biased and class-based policing in western democracies really is, you need only attend a hunt. The fact they still felt the need to employ even more protection – at their own expense this time - underlines perfectly how impactful the Hunt Sabotage movement has been.

ACT YOUR RAGE- above - *A Policeman and a Brixton Hunt Saboteur discuss the finer points of trespass law under the recently introduced Criminal Justice Act, (CJA) of 1994, Surrey Union Hunt circa mid- 1990's.*

The CJA was introduced by the Tories to address the thriving Rave scene, New Age Traveller movement and hunt sabotage. The Act gave the police new powers to arrest for trespass but was so badly designed that Police forces around the UK, particularly Essex Police, found themselves getting sued by the very people they were hoping to subdue – some hunt sabs received tens of thousands in compensation for wrongful arrest and illegal detention. In fact, the UK Police were one of the largest financial donors to the Hunt Saboteurs at this time. Use of the Act was soon deemed unaffordable by most Forces. source HSA archive.

By the early 1980's, hunt sabotage had spread its wings.

First mention of it in Ireland is in 1983 when Saboteurs from around the UK joined Dublin activists for four days of sabotage. Twenty Saboteurs successfully hit the Tara Harriers, West Meath Foxhounds, Louth Foxhounds and Goldburn Beagles despite violence and threats from enraged Hunters and their support. The West Meath hunt were the most aggressive, with 7 sabs getting attacked by a mob of 40 hunt supporters.

Hunt Sabotage around Belfast and Dublin became commonplace from then on. Fellow sabs from around Britain often travelled over to help out and skill share. In 1994 more groups from the West and South of the country sprang up, including a Galway group that I helped form.

My first engagement with the anti-blood sports movement was in the mid 1980's. The Irish Council Against Blood Sports (ICABS) asked me to paint a large banner stating "only rotter's kill otters" to hang on their float in the upcoming St. Patricks day parade. I duly obliged.

ICABS also organized protests at Clonmel Coursing track at its annual Coursing championships and had shown some inititive when they blocked the entrance to the Clubs car park in 1987. The Police had to arrest them to protect them from the angry mob of Coursers who threatened to tear the activists limb from limb. This made the RTE news that evening and inspired me and fellow punks to join the following years march. We were keen to repeat the previous year's action, but ICABS made it clear this would not be happening. Once was enough. They had stuck their heads above the parapet and were terrified by the aggressive reaction. So we all stood on one side of a road and waved banners and shouted slogans at jeering, triumphant blood sports enthusiasts as they made their way unhindered into the stadium. It was all very tokenistic and disempowering.

ICABS were the only game in town when it came to campaigning against blood sports but were unfortunately hobbled by their intrinsic conservativism. At a later ICABS meeting I suggested to the local branch organizer we use hunt sabotage as a way to shift the dial on the debate. He was an approachable fellow but also a Fine Gael Councillor. He rejected the idea as too controversial for the public to accept. It was silent vigils and placard waving from now on, with the occasional letter to the Press.

No longer happy to work with a group we considered ineffective, us punks left and did what we did best – form bands and play to our friends in tiny venues around Cork city. We sang the praises of direct action and anarchy, looking to Britain for inspiration and lamenting our societies indifference to animal suffering.

In 1993 I was living in Edinburgh. Hunt Saboteurs were active in the city, part of the wider anarcho punk milieu, and I joined in. My first hunt sabotage was outside Edinburgh, and it was all very confusing. The idea is to gain control of the hounds and direct them to areas already covered by the hunt. This is done by using horn calls and voice calls, imitating the Master of Foxhounds. When performed by a skilled saboteur, the effects are immediate – the pack of hounds will at the very least become confused and stop in their tracks, at best they will retreat over ground they have just gone over, toward the sound of the Saboteurs' calls. Blowing a coherent sound through a hunting bugle is quite hard and takes practice.

A much easier way to command the hound's attention is to play an audio recording of the hounds "on cry' through a megaphone. The sound of hounds *on cry* is the excited yelp they bark out *en masse* when they've discovered the scent of a quarry. Dogs reflexively react to this sound and come running when they hear it. This is remarkably effective and perfectly sabotages the hunting process. The confused and scattered dogs must be gathered back together again, and this takes time. Time not spent hunting.

The other main tactic in the sabotage handbook was to arrive at the hunting area really early in the morning, before the Hunt arrive, and pre-spray woods and copses' with citronella-laced water to smother the scent of foxes.

Being new on the scene, I was content to largely watch and observe. The hunt would disappear into a woods, we would follow them, they'd move off at a gallop as soon as we arrived, and so on. Police were about in a couple of cars but didn't wish to get wet and muddy so left us and the Hunt to it. I don't recall them catching a fox and I was impressed by the persistency of the Saboteurs – our presence kept the hunt moving quickly through the area as they sought to stay ahead of us. Simply showing up was enough to alter the course of the days hunt.

A few months later, I decided to hitch south with a friend to Newcastle in the north England for a sabotage of the annual Northumberland Beagling Festival, a week-long get-together for 'Open Hare' Coursing enthusiasts nationwide.

Open hare coursing differs from Park hare coursing in that it takes place over a wide, open area of land rather than within an enclosed course as typically happens in Ireland. It's like a foxhunt but the hunters are all on foot and their victim is a hare. The Northumberland Beagling Festival had been receiving attention from Saboteurs every year for the previous 6 years and was beginning to crack under the strain of it all. The number of days spent Coursing, and the frequency of each days Coursing races, was reducing each year and this year, 1993, was to be their last.

We arrived in Newcastle after an easy hitch down and called round to the address I had been given by Saboteurs in Edinburgh. A Mohican'd Punk answered the door and let us in. The house was occupied by a group of 5 Punks, all experienced in the art of hunt sabotage. Friendly and welcoming, we were invited to sit down and make ourselves comfortable. I was determined to learn what I could about sabbing an open hare coursing event and began asking questions. "There won't be much tactical sabotage over the next week" explained one of the punks. "Our main strategy is to increase the cost of the security requirements for the hunters, by maintaining a presence and making an occasional foray toward where the hunt is operating. We never get far because they employ dozens of squaddies and local heavies to stop us from getting near the hunt. This protects them in the short term but at great expense. We sabotage this event by financially draining them. This year we estimate they are spending $11 K for security. The Coursers and their hired thugs are violent and the police usually hostile too, but we know we're having an effect. This is a nationwide call out so there will be dozens of saboteurs out most days. It's gonna be fun."

The next day it began. We left Newcastle in the early morning. In a convoy of vehicles about ten strong, we drove to where the hare coursers were meeting. It was the deep countryside, a network of fields separated by thick lines of trees, narrow country lanes criss-crossing the land. We formed up in a large group and eyed up the security – 100 or men, some of whom were Squaddies from a nearby garrison. Our tactics varied. Initially we split into small groups and wandered around the area seeking weaknesses in the security that circled an area of land as the hunt moved through it. Every so often we'd mob up and walk in a long line straight toward an equally long line of security. When the two lines met it was a game of bulldog as we tried to run around or through the mess of people. We never made it through but that wasn't the point – sustaining the need for serious security was the point.

And on it went, 6 hours a day for 4 days. Injuries were sustained on both sides; some arrests were made and the hunt was, by and large, not interfered with. One day a carload of American tourists stopped by to see what was happening – their quiet spin around the gentle English countryside had suddenly erupted into a scene of chaos. Dozens of crusties and punks were slugging it out with paramilitary looking security as police violently arrested saboteurs, and a pack of hounds howled in the distance." What's going on here buddy?" the driver enquired of me as I was running past their car. "It's about hares" I replied and trotted on to join the fray.

Buckling under the financial strain imposed by the saboteurs, the Northumberland Beagling Festival has never occurred since, forced out of existence by the relentless pressure of the HSA.

BACK IN BLACK - SABOTAGING A BEAGLING PACK, above, *where the hunters themselves are on foot, is a lot easier than sabbing a foxhunt. Here, the saboteurs (on the left, looking happy, dressed in black) 'escort' the Four Shires Beagle pack (on the right, looking glum, dressed in beige) back home after a successfull days sabotage, East England, 1992..*

Effective, or certainly enjoyable hunting is practically impossibly under these circumstances. Unlike Hunt Sabotage, which is highly effective and tremendous fun under these circumstances.

A Hunt and it's sabotage could go all day until it gets dark, or more typically mere minutes if they decide to pack up and go home. Or they might explode with frustrated rage and begin attacking people. The close proximity of the sabs with the Hunt meant violence was an ever-present threat. Any significant aggression from the Hunt means they will be on the receiving end of a 'regional' or 'national' hit, when dozens, maybe hundreds, of Sabs descend on the Hunt the following week. Don't underestimate the good, good times you can have doing animal activism like this. Some of the most exciting, scary, exhilarating, intimidating, powerful and bonding experiences I've ever had have been out Sabbing.

Image from 'Sabotage – the story of the Hunt Saboteurs Association' '

"Currently most beagle packs go home if sabs or monitors are present. This is the safe and sensible course of action. What is not acceptable is to carry on regardless with them all around you as if they weren't there. Even if your hunt has never seen sabs before, sooner or later they will turn up." Sound advice from none other than Richard Tyacke, Director of the Associatoon of Harriers and Beagles (UK), 2020.

Later that year I moved to Galway, Irelands bohemian capital.

One evening I attended a public meeting by ICABS. A good chance to meet others who might be interested in sabbing, I thought.

The meeting was well attended, maybe 40 or so. During the Q&A at the end, I asked if ICABS would consider hunt sabotage as a tactic. A firm "**NO** "was the reply, followed by a denouncement of the HSA as a hooligan organization, 'setting the movement back years.' I defended the tactic, explaining I had recent experience of sabbing in the UK and could affirm that it is the hunt and their followers who are typically guilty of violence against sabs. "And if anyone here is interested in taking effective direct action against the local hunt, join me in the bar after this meeting for a chat."

Then I left the room, I'd heard enough from ICABS for one evening. I settled in for a few pints and when the meeting ended, two women from the city's Animal Rights group took me up on the offer.

Their local campaign was small but persistent. They had an information stall every Saturday in the city centre and held the occasional demo whenever a circus was in town. They were both interested in hunt sabbing but had no experience of it.

I immediately got involved in the group. We were informally affiliated with the Dublin-based Alliance for Animal Rights (AFAR) and received leaflets and posters from them, along with literature from London Greenpeace and Animal Aid.

In 1994, there was a weekend conference on the art and science of hunt sabotage, hosted by "Dynamite" Dave Nelson and others from the Belfast Hunt Saboteurs. Dave had only recently been released from a 3-and-a-half-year prison sentence for bombing hunters' vehicles and was now an above-ground anti-hunt activist, keen to spread the tactic around the Country.

100 or so people attended and we learned how to effectively disrupt fox hunts using horn and voice calls and false scents. We also learned how to handle hostile Police and hunt aggression – both guaranteed to be encountered. A relatively new weapon – the gizmo – was also introduced. The gizmo was simply a tape recording of a pack

of hounds on cry – yelping excitedly – played through a hand -held speaker. This was a very effective way of grabbing and commanding the attention of the actual pack of hounds at a hunt. Assuming a fox has been sighted, the hounds come running to the source of the sound only to find a grinning dreadlocked crusty holding a gizmo. This device negated the need to have a practiced horn-blower in the ranks. Proper horn blowing is quite hard to master. Anyone could operate a gizmo.

Dublin activists had already gained hunt sabotage experience by going to Belfast on weekends and sabbing there with the local Belfast group.

Our Galway group would now do the same with the Dublin group, then strike out on our own when ready.

So a few weeks after the conference, a few of us travelled again to Dublin. A foot-based mink hunt pack were selected for attention and two dozen Saboteurs travelled out of the city to put theory into practice. Because they weren't on horseback, they were easy to follow and keep up with. We had not announced our visit and the hunters initially presumed we were supporters. When we pulled out the gizmo and took control of the hounds, they quickly realized our intentions. They were caught on the hop, and we so confused and misdirected the days hunting that they packed up a after a few hours and left. No aggression, no shouted threats, just a quick, bemused, and wordless withdrawal.

We now turned our attention to our own back yard in Galway, mainly the Galway Blazers foxhunt.

In late 1994, fellow sabs from Dublin joined the nascent Galway Hunt Saboteurs on our first foray against the Blazers.

The Galway saboteurs were made up of the local animal rights group, people from a nearby "new age traveller" site and associated friends. Including our Dublin comrades, we numbered about 15. Some of us had previous experience of sabbing in the UK but most were inexperienced.

As we slowly drove into the Hunts meet up village (Ardrahan) in a small convoy of vehicles, the hunt knocked their whiskies and champagne back and trotted off before we had time to disembark and gather our forces.

Now, the Irish Master of Foxhounds Association publishs a book in advance of each hunting season of the differing meet-up points for each Hunt around the Country. A Hunt likes to spread itself around a given area and each week has a different meet up point, typically a village with suitable hunting territory nearby. This almanac is readily available in most bookstores and gave us time to plot our moves before each sab.

We had identified a high hill of rough land that was bang in the middle of the days likely hunting area.

We watched the hunt speed off, followed by quad bikes and cars with supporters in them, but rather than give chase we drove straight to the hill and observed the hunt begin to flush hounds through a copse of trees below us.

Out with the Gizmo and on with the tape. Through binoculars I saw the lead hounds sniffing ground before them as they sought a scent. Suddenly they stopped and their ears pricked up as they tuned into the recoded sounds of fellow beagle dogs on cry in the distance. The lead dogs turned and ran up the hill toward the sound, followed by a barking pack of 30 or so hounds.

When they got to the top and found us, they stopped and looked utterly perplexed. Some began sniffing frantically on the ground, others wandered aimlessly with heads high in the air.

Slowly the hounds disappeared back into the foliage seeking their masters.

The Hunt regathered their pack and pushed forward toward other woods when we turned on the Gizmo again. Hounds once more came running up the hill. Keeping a tight pack of hounds in a spearhead formation is vital to efficient hunting and we were tearing that formation apart with the Gizmo.

This kept happening. We repeated the trick a half dozen more times, undisturbed by the hunt or their thuggish support. We barely even saw them.

Dusk falls early in Irelands Autumn and the Hunt were packed up and gone by mid-afternoon.

We were elated that our first hunt sabotage had gone so well. it was textbook sabbing – sabotage by stealth, 100% effective, zero violence.

A month later we were back, again with Dublin comrades to boost numbers.

This time their location did not give many clues as to which way they would head off, so we decided to go straight to their meet and follow them on foot when they moved. Arriving at the meet up village, the Blazers and their supporters initially thought we were either passing through or were hunt supporters. When we climbed out of the vehicles, it quickly dawned on them we were the hated "Anti's".

Everyone milled about as the mounted hunters sipped from flutes of champagne and as soon as they began setting off, we followed them and managed to block the path ahead of them. Our mass of bodies scared the horses from going forward. With rising anger, the lead hunters rammed their horses into us, only adding to the general air of confusion as Sabs ducked to avoid riding crops and whips aimed at us.

Bear in mind the only people on the hunt who could *actually hunt* comprise of a half dozen or so riders. The rest – another twenty or more – simply follow along, "enjoying the chase" as it were. So, when they saw this violence unfolding, they didn't know what to do. Most hung back, frozen in hesitation. Some, probably all, had heard of encounters between Saboteurs and hunts all over the UK. Tales told of massive fights erupting that sent many on both sides to the hospital. Now this was happening here, to their own hunt.

The Master of Foxhounds then lead his posse down a bridle path and away from the fracas. We followed on foot. Using their superior speed, they presumed they could put enough space between us and them.

The Gizmo was produced by one of the Dublin sabs and was immediately successful, bringing the hounds back toward us, yelping in expectation.

The hunt turned back and galloped into us, forcing us into hedgerows and fields on either side of the path. Some of the hunt followed us into the fields and bashed a few of us with their riding crops, causing nasty gashes on the heads and faces of some sabs. They were beside themselves at this point, unsure of what to do and reacting with feral violence. Horses were being used as weapons, shoving, and ramming into people. Our vehicles suffered light damage too.

With their height, weight and speed, the mounted horse is surely natures Sherman tank. A skilled rider with a whip or riding crop has every advantage over any enemy on foot, making the skull an easy target for striking.

The hunt then retreated *en masse* back to their meet-up point in the village and had a hurried discussion amongst themselves as we also regrouped and nursed our wounds. We watched with delight as they summoned their horse boxes and hound van, packed up and went home. Their impotent fury was visible in their faces as they drove past us, defeated, and enraged.

Our third time was not so lucky....

Early morning on the 19th of January 1995, we set off again for another day's sabotage. True to form, Dublin sabs joined us, bulking our numbers up to about 20 people.

We made our way in a small convoy to the Galway Blazers meet-up point, a village in East Galway called Dunsandle, about a half-hour drive from Galway city.

Our plan that day was thus – half of us, me included, were to pursue the hunt on foot. The remainder would drive in two cars to points well ahead of the hunt and lay down citronella spray to cover up any fox scents.

I had borrowed a camcorder, hoping this might act as a deterrent against aggression and as a means to record anything of worth that day.

The Hunt soon moved off down a narrow lane.

Six of us followed behind, jogging to keep up.

After about 5 minutes we all ended up in a large field and the hunt came to a sudden stop. Riders fanned out around the field and quickly formed a ring around us, blocking any way out.

A dozen or so huntsmen dismounted and ran into us, whips and riding crops raining down on us. They made a concentrated attack on me as I had the camera. Before I got punched and kicked to the ground, I managed to hurl the camera, recording all the time, to another saboteur. He was immediately set upon and had the camera taken from him.

Once they had the camera they withdrew and galloped off in pursuit of the other sabs who had fled the field.

I got up and ran back the way we had come. I was on my own at this point – people had scattered in all directions once the attack began and were now in various adjacent fields being chased by the Hunt. Screaming and shouting were coming from all directions as they laid into Saboteurs.

As I ran back up the path toward Dunsandle, I saw a police car parked at the end of the lane, the three cops inside watching me approach. I could hear and feel the sound of horses coming behind me at a pace, the ground shaking as they bore down on me. When a bunch of hunt supporters ran past the police car and toward me, I knew I had to get off the lane, hedged in as it was by stone walls on both sides.

I hopped over the right-hand side wall and straight into another confrontation – two hunt support were laying into Gary, a fellow Sab. One had him by the hoodie as his mate was aiming punches to the back of his head.

I ran as fast as I could into the mass of bodies and began punching one attacker in the face as we all fell over in a writhing heap. Gary and I were up like a shot and ran toward the village and, we hoped, safety.

We got to the village with its police car and its angry locals, who lined the street shouting abuse at us. The three cops in their car didn't get out or make eye contact with us.

We saw the other Saboteurs at the far end of the small village and began walking down the middle of the main road toward them as the police car slowly followed behind. Hunt supporters emerged from the crowd and variously kicked and punched us, as the police idly watched on, until we reached our fellow Sabs in their now battered cars.

They hadn't fared any better – as they tried to drive out of the village after the Hunt, they were stopped by a few dozen locals and supporters. The screaming mob initially tried to roll the cars but couldn't get the necessary momentum to turn them so settled on dancing the pogo on the car roofs instead. Some tried to punch their way through the car windows to take the stills camera one of the Sabs had. Side view mirrors were broken off and panels were dented. The attack subsided when more police cars began arriving into the village.

If the crowd had thought they would have got away with lynching us they would have.

The assault caused a stir in the local media and I tried bringing a prosecution against the Hunt. Even though it took place in front of three policemen and having written testimonies from a dozen people assaulted that day, The Director of Public Prosecutions decided there wasn't enough evidence to go forward.

We couldn't afford any legal representation so couldn't do anything about it.

Hunt Sabotage against the Galway Blazers was put on freeze following the violence. However, since 2019 the Blazers have been receiving attention from the Connacht Hunt Saboteurs who continue to use direct action in defence of wildlife. They also continue getting attacked by the Blazers, who still aren't being prosecuted for it.

Indeed, hunt sabotage is now a part of the landscape in Ireland, with a group in each province actively saving wildlife with peaceful direct action throughout the year.

In all my years sabotaging foxhunts, one other incident rivalled the ambush in Galway for sheer ferocity but this time the steel-toed boot was very much on the other foot. Shortly after the incident in Galway with the Blazers, I moved to Hertfordshire, just north of London and quickly got involved with the **CHILTERN HUNT SABOTEURS,** who had been sabbing the Vale of Aylesbury Fox Hunt for years. In fact, the Vale of Aylesbury had borne the brunt of a lot of the first wave of militant direct action for animals in the early 1970's. Ronnie Lee, founder of the ALF, lived nearby in Luton, and was a frequent presence at their hunts. He developed the Band of Mercy tactics of vandalizing hunters' vehicles on the Vale and nearby hunts. When the Vale of Aylesbury Hunt sent in the heavies to teach the sabs a lesson, Lee spearheaded the violent counter-reaction to their violence and eventually the Hunt and their thugs backed off, leading to an uneasy peace between the two groups, allowing the sabs to continue sabbing with less fear of attack. The Vale had been getting persistently sabbed for about 25 years by the time I joined in, and by this point usually kept to a policy of no-communication with Sabs.

Despite this largely peaceful co-existence, there was one small group of terrier men who enjoyed driving about in their flash 4x4 seeking lone Sabs to intimidate and attack. Led by a hardman called Roderick Wilson, a 39-year-old gamekeeper, their modus operandi was to speed up behind a lost lone Sab or two, hop out, give them a kicking then speed off again, horn beeping. The Hunt pretended to not know them and the Police were not interested.

Word about Roderick and his merry men had gotten out to other Sab groups in and around the greater London area, including the notoriously spikey Brixton Hunt Saboteurs.

So, on Saturday morning on 21st March 1998, when most other Hunts in the country had packed up for the season, the Vale of Aylesbury foxhunt had a very unwelcome visit from Sabs from across the southeast region, all eager to remind the hunt that violence against saboteurs would not be tolerated. The local Sab group (us) had not called for a regional hit but here it was, unfolding before our eyes. The Vale was the only hunt still going out this late in the season and were perhaps, once again, due some heavy manners....

As more and more black clad Saboteurs arrived at the meet-up point in beaten-up ford transits with metal grills over the windshields and punk rock blaring, the Hunt must also have known this was not to be a typical day out. As they sipped from flutes of champagne, eyes darting nervously, around them milled dozens of menacing, aggressive balaclava'd anarchists spoiling for a fight, with more arriving by the minute. Soon the Saboteurs numbered a hundred or so.

Nevertheless, the Master of Foxhounds decided to carry on with the days hunting, trusting the local Constabulary would keep on top of things……

MASTER BAIT - Scuffles between hunt Supporters and Sabs began almost immediately, but the real violence took place an hour into the hunting. Roderick, out on bail for assaulting a Sab some months before, and his mates weren't put off by the arrival of this new element and set off on a familiar little hunt of their own. As they meandered down the lanes of the Buckinghamshire countryside they stumbled upon their quarry – three 'lost-looking', out-of-area Sabs, peering at a map.

The bait was set.

Speeding up to them, Roderick stopped the 4x4 with a jolt and he and his fellow thugs hopped out, iron bars in hand ready to teach these Sabs a lesson they would never forget. As the three unarmed Saboteurs pleaded for restraint, Roderick moved in first, hitting a female saboteur over the head with an iron bar when suddenly everything went black- 40 fellow Sabs had been waiting/'lost' in a nearby copse and suddenly emerged, rushing to help their comrades. Roderick was quickly surrounded, disarmed, and his weapon was used, with gusto, against him and his chums.

All three hunt thugs were quickly beaten to the ground and kept there with repeated blows to the head and body by their own weapons. Their vehicle was then completely smashed up – all windows broken, bodywork dented, and tyres slashed. The saboteurs departed, leaving three jack-knifed thugs writhing in pain on the ground next to a devastated and deflated 4x4.

Try explaining that one to the AA.

FACE-LIFT - Roderick was hospitalized for 3 months with broken nose and face bones, and images of his battered-sideways mug was used as anti-Sab propaganda by the Countryside Alliance on their website for years after.

As a result of the violence, a commission including MP's Michael Heseltine, John Bercow (Speaker of the House of Commons) and local Police and Hunters was formed to investigate how the Police lost control that day and to prevent a repeat. Police arrested 18 saboteurs, but all charges were dropped.

Superintendent Paul Friday, Aylesbury Police area commander said that Police had been "managing a very fluid situation which involved hunt supporters and opposing demonstrators in many separate incidents." that day.

Roderick was rarely seen at a Vale of Aylesbury foxhunt again. When he did attend, he kept his distance and never gave us trouble.

above - *Saboteurs 'debate' with the Crawley and Horsham Hunt, Sussex, UK, circa 1996. Mass clashes frequently erupted in otherwise quiet country lanes between hunt supporters and saboteurs throughout the 1980's and 90's. image from Squall #12, p.27, photo by Andrew Testa.*

FOX TALES

Hunts usually packed up or refused to even start hunting once they clocked a long convoy of Sab vehicles coming their way. In 1999, again at the end of the season, we joined forces with Saboteurs from across London and the South East and embarked on a little tour of the countryside. Beginning early in the morning at the Vale of Aylesbury hunt, we parked up en masse outside their kennels, 100 saboteurs in a dozen battered old Land Rovers and Sherpa Vans. The two coppers on duty had a few rushed conversations with the Master of Foxhounds and over their police radios and sensibly concluded, that, given the circumstances they could not guarantee the Hunts safety. They ordered the Hunt to stay home for the day. This was particularly infuriating for them as the last meet of the season is meant to be a bit of an occasion, like the Boxing Day hunt.

One-Nil, and we didn't even have to leave the comfort of our Land Rovers.

Leaving a vehicle behind with a few Sabs to monitor the Vale in case they changed their minds (they didn't), we sped on to the next target, coiling like an angry black snake along winding country lanes.

WE soon arrived at exclusive Eton College, resplendent with a large imposing gate and walls. Set in a beautiful woodland, this prestigious establishment, training ground for the next elite, had its very own beagling pack which hadn't been sabbed in some time. WE parked up in a long row outside the massive gates, forming a solid wall of vehicles, and waited. It's all about creating that first impression....

After a few minutes we heard the sound of excited young men and their dogs, led by a Lecturer, as they made their way toward us. They were completely oblivious to our presence and froze in their tracks when they suddenly noticed a huge mob of black-attired, masked-up activists standing on and around ten vehicles, blocking their path and showing no intent of moving.

The teacher leading the procession, in effect their Master of Hounds, slowly approached the gate and enquired if we were Saboteurs. Yes, came the reply.

He immediately turned back to his students, and they quickly and quietly went back the way they had come. A half-hour went past until one lone copper drove past, parked up nearby and eyed us for a bit and then left as well.

Two-Nil to the Saboteurs.

One vehicle remained at the gates to monitor for any sneaky hunting and the rest of us left once more to Carry On Sabbing.

As we were driving to the next target, we spotted a trio of shooters blasting away at birds from their pop-up camouflage 'hide' in the middle of a field.

Dozens of Sabs jumped out of their transport and made directly toward them, catching them completely off-guard and unprepared. Camouflage equipment was removed from them and broken into pieces, the pheasants they had just shot were taken and buried and the three unhappy Shooters were enthusiastically escorted back to their vehicles and sent on their merry way. They never said a word as all this happened to them and offered no resistance and it was over in ten minutes. I got the feeling this had happened to them before, perhaps more than once.

Three-Nil.

We carried on to our final target, the notoriously aggressive Surrey Union Foxhunt, and arrived as they were in full swing. Hounds were 'on cry' and dozens of mounted hunters and their support on foot were barrelling after a tiny figure in the distance. Some sabs on foot were keeping pace with the hunt.

After quickly consulting with the Surrey sabs, the convoy split up and went in different directions. Unsure of where the hunt was heading, our land rover, packed with ten saboteurs, headed down a narrow lane for about ten minutes until we were forced to halt - a hunt supporter was blocking the lane with his car and showed no signs of moving.

One of ours got out of the land rover, walked over to him, and requested he move his car. "Fuck off" was the reply.

I then walked over to his car, repeating the request. His already-ugly face twisted in hate as he punched me square in the face from his sitting position. I immediately punched him back, landing my fist right on his nose. He began closing the door window as I continued to punch his head and then the glass of the door as it went up. He lurched forward in his car, reversed, and then sped forward. He drove past our land rover and straight toward another Sab, Jack, who was running to help me. Jack jumped clear just in time and the hunt supporter drove straight into a ditch, breaking his headlights in the process. Reversing his car furiously back onto the lane, the rear window was smashed through by Jack using a full bottle of citronella spray. He then sped forward again, disappearing round the corner with slightly less car than when he first got here.

It was like the wild west, or the west of Ireland.

We then received word over the CB that the Hunt were returning to their meet point, presumably to pack up and go home. Surrounded by groups of mobile Saboteurs in every direction, including the spiky 'Brixton Mob', the Surrey Union had been advised to call it a day by the local Constabulary, who were once again unable to guarantee safety.

All in all, a brilliant day's work.

THE MOB RULES - **Quantity has a quality all of its own** – above - *Brixton Sabs* in *action circa early 1990's. Each sab group has its own approach to sabotage. Tactics varied according to sab numbers and the likelihood of violence from the hunt and their supporters. Brixton's approach was to swamp hunts with numbers and aggression was used to counter violence from the hunt fraternity. Led largely by anarchist squatters and anti-fascists militants, they were regularly called upon to assist other sab groups in countering aggression from the Hunt. source HSA archive.*

UPDATE – The Vale of Aylesbury Foxhunt no longer exist – they merged with the Garth and South Berks Foxhunt in 2002 to form a new Hunt called the Kimblewick Hunt. Since hunting became a significant issue in the 1970's, support for the practice has steadily declined, leading to less money, forcing many dozens of Hunts to fold or merge and rebrand. When the HSA began life in late 1963, the were 250 registered Foxhunts in the United Kingdom. As of mid-2023, this number stands at about 187 and continues to fall. Of course, since the ban in 2004, all such hunting in the England and Wales (Scotland banned Hunting in 2002) must by law only be trail- also called drag- hunting, where the hounds seek and then follow a scent laid by a person using a scented rag, no killing involved. But the ban wasn't the End of hunting, only the Beginning of the End, as the hunting fraternity carried on chasing down and killing wildlife, openly breaking the new Law with impunity. In stark contrast to their previous approach to dealing with hunt saboteurs, the Police decided they weren't interested and were nowhere to be seen. Hunt Saboteurs became hunt monitors and working with other groups like the RSPCA and LACS, are now involved in doing the job the Police are apparently so reluctant to do – protecting wildlife and prosecuting wildlife criminals and countryside vandals. Drones and high-quality surveillance equipment makes it possible to spot for any deliberate signs of hunting and provide vital evidence in the Courts.

When Saboteurs or Hunt Monitors show up these days, the hunters have to pretend to be trail hunting. Typically, they simply pack up and go home. With no Police around to protect them, and no interest in Trail hunting, they retreat.

IN 2020, the UK's foxhunting body, the Hunting Office, held a training webinar for 150 of their supporters. During the discussions, various influential faces in the organisation talked about how to use trail-hunting as a smokescreen for 'traditional' (i.e. illegal) hunting, using birds of prey to flush out foxes, using 'burner' phones to avoid leaving evidence, how to handle interviews with the police - "There are no friendly interviews with police officers' advises the meetings Chair, Lord Mancroft, at one point – and what to do when Saboteurs turn up ("Go home" advised one). We know all this because the webinar was leaked to the Hunt Saboteurs Association and was used as evidence that Hunting packs all over the UK were routinely breaking the Law. As a result, huge Landowners in the UK such as National Trust, United Utilities, Forestry England and the Lake District National Park Authority, and others, all suspended hunting licences on their land. Mark Hankinson, the Director of the Master of Foxhounds Association, was charged with intentionally encouraging others to commit illegal acts and donations to the Hunt Saboteurs Association soared.

Hankinson was found guilty in 2021 but had the verdict overturned on appeal when he managed to convince the Courts he was never intending anyone break the law, it was about fooling saboteurs.

A small victory for the Hunters perhaps but they are clearly losing the war – hunting for 'fun' (or *Funting*)is on the back foot and in terminal decline in the UK. They face legal, logistical and cultural barriers that get ever higher over time. The Scottish Parliament lead the way on this, recently banning Trail Hunting because it was being used as a smokescreen for illegal hunting for years. This spells the end for the Hunting fraternity in Scotland. Even the 200 plus year old County Down Stag Hunt in the North of Ireland announced its collapse in July 2023. There are now no stag Hunts at all in the UK or Ireland.

Hunt Saboteurs are now also regularly active in France, Australia and Sweden and, of course, Ireland.

THE GANGS ALL HERE – above - *Hunt Saboteurs descend en masse on the Surrey Union Foxhunt circa 1991.Once a flagship outfit, by the early 1990's the Union had become a laughingstock amongst the Hunting fraternity. Nearby Hunts would pass on details of the Unions upcoming meets to the HSA so we would target the Union and leave the other hunts alone. The HSA estimated 80% of the Unions meets were sabotaged around this time. Their hounds were at this point basically useless, and the sabs were better at controlling them than the ever-changing line up of huntsmen. source HSA archive.*

above – police wrestle with saboteurs as entitled hunters look on. Tynedale Foxhounds, circa 1993. Foxhunters often lorded it over the local constabulary, telling them what to do and how to do it. source HSA archive

Of course, vocal opposition to hunting is as old and 'traditional' as hunting itself.

GOD TOLD HIM NOT TO DO IT – The story goes that one day an avid Hunter named Hubert, born into nobility in France in 656 AD, was chasing a Stag in the Ardennes forest when the Stag suddenly stopped and turned and, as a white cross shone between his great antlers, spoke to Hubert and said : "Hubert unless thou turnest to the Lord and leadest a holy life, thou shalt quickly go down into Hell."

139

The huntsman immediately resolved to forgo hunting, condemning it as an act against God. He became an ordained priest and then the Bishop of Liege in 708AD. It is said that local clergy have been forbidden to partake in hunting ever since Hubert's ordination. Hubert died in 727 AD and was canonized (made saint) in 1744.

Coincidentally, it was witnessing the gory culmination of a stag hunt, over twelve centuries later, that inspired the formation of the Hunt Saboteurs Association in merry old England in the year of our lord 1963.

The Hunting fraternity, particularly in France, Germany and Belgium, hijacked Saint Hubert and his anti-hunting stance and warped his legacy into a sanctimonious, self-serving icon of what they call 'ethical' sport hunting. They venerate him as their saint protector, as though *they're* the ones who need protection. Shouldn't their patron saint be Satan?

Some of them even wear the St Hubert medal for safety and luck. The only protection these creeps need is from each other - Hunters (particularly for some reason in France) often mistake fellow hunters for 'prey' and eagerly shoot each other, which happens more often than you think (but less often than it should). The National Office of Hunting and Wildlife estimate hunters in France alone shot and killed 400 people over the last 20 years. Fortunately, the vast majority of the victims were other hunters, but innocent hikers, cyclists, even sunbathers and many others have also been killed. 3000 have been injured.

There are St Hubert's Orders, hunting clubs, Cathedrals, paintings, beers, hotels, medals, food producers (gravy), restaurants, streets, towns, airports, statues of both stag and saint (separate and together), hell, he's even got his own feast day (November 3rd). Perversely, this day represents the start of the hunting season in Europe. And its World Vegan Month! Cheeky bastards. St. Hubert would be spinning in his grave, if his grave hadn't been dug up in 825 and transferred to Belgium, until what remained was exhumed *again* sometime during the Reformation in the 15th century and subsequently lost to history. Rest In Peace? Not this guy.

The stag-with-cross logo is used all over the place - t-shirts, tattoos, Jägermeister ('master hunter') liquor, you've probably seen the image a thousand times without realising it's from a story about a talking stag who denounces hunting to anyone within earshot who's eaten enough magic mushrooms.

I'm happy to report Hubert is getting finally just recognition with his own Award recognising *"individuals who have given up activities that exploit animals to become examples of compassionate living.*" I'm less happy to report that the Award is presented by the Catholic Concern for Animals (CCA) movement but if nothing else it illustrates the diverse range of emphasis within Catholicism. Formally known as the Catholic Association for the Defence of Animals, the group make a brief appearance in this books Diary of Actions chapter – in March 1987, they joined forces with the Irish Council Against Blood Sports in a demonstration outside Clonmel Police Station. Both groups accused the local Gardai of conspiring with the local hunting fraternity to squash any opposition to 'bloodsports' in the region, in particular Coursing. Specifically, they highlighted how Irish Council Against Bloodsports Chairman, Pat Phelan, was being targeted by Gardai – he had been arrested and held for interrogation about recent ALF activity at least twice over this period. This is the only time the Catholic Association for the Defence of Animals held a demonstration, as far as the public record shows. Gardai described the accusations of collusion as "Rubbish".

Despite their, and the CCA's, genteel conservatism, they now promote vegan living and oppose factory farming and hunting. 2021's St. Hubert Award went to Irishman Randal Plunket, AKA Lord Dunsany, 21st Baron of the 1700-acre, 11th century Dunsany Estate and Castle, a man who counts amongst his ancestors another saint, Saint Oliver Plunket.

Randal inherited the title of Lord Dunsany when his father passed in 2011 and subsequently founded Dunsany Nature Reserve, Ireland's first vegan rewilding project. In 2014, animal agriculture was abandoned and all 750-acres of fields that once contained farm animals were left to rewild. Limited commercial crop growing continues but most of his Estate is now either native forest or ex-pastoral land reclaimed for rewilding. Lord Randal also banned hunting on his land, including the local foxhunt who had been hunting there for decades. A committed vegan, Randal enjoys Death Metal and making horror movies in his spare time. Praise the Lord!

above -*The last few Hunts of the season in March often saw variations on traditional hunt sabotage tactics. Here we are blockading the hunt vehicles inside their kennels. That's **me** in the image above, grey face mask, standing in front of the hounds van as they try to begin the days hunting, Vale of Aylesbury Hunt, Aylesbury, circa 1999. We held them up for hours, until enough police arrived to convince us to cease the blockade and allow the Hunt through. They arrested one of ours for obstruction and a melee broke out, delaying the Hunts progress for another 20 minutes as police and sabs tried to arrest and de-arrest someone at the same time. Narrow country lanes aren't really built for this sort of thing.source Authors personal collection.*

above – *a few hours later and the local, just-out-of-bed constabulary arrive. 'Wots all this ere then?'. That's me, back to the camera, bottom right. source Authors personal collection.*

HUNTING MAKES US CROSS (DRESS) – above - *Once, after a few too many beers, we decided to turn up at the next Vale of Aylesbury hunt dressed in drag to emphasise drag hunting as an alternative to fox hunting. A bunch of punks and skinheads, all in dressed and wigs, marched into the field the hunt were meeting in carrying a large banner that read "time to turn to drag, ducky" and "Hunting makes us cross (dress)". Some of us stayed in drag the whole day, despite fights with Support and scuffles with cops. Our tenacity earned us a slot of News at Ten and wolf whistling from Constabulary. source Authors personal collecti*

LONG ARMS OF THE LAW – above - *fellow Hunt Saboteur **Chesh** defies arrest and keeps struggling with these cops for about 15 minutes, pushing them off him and wrapping himself round a pole until they eventually managed to handcuff him and get him into a police car. The Charge was Aggravated Trespass. circa 1998, Vale of Aylesbury hunt, somewhere in Hertfordshire. source Authors personal collection.*

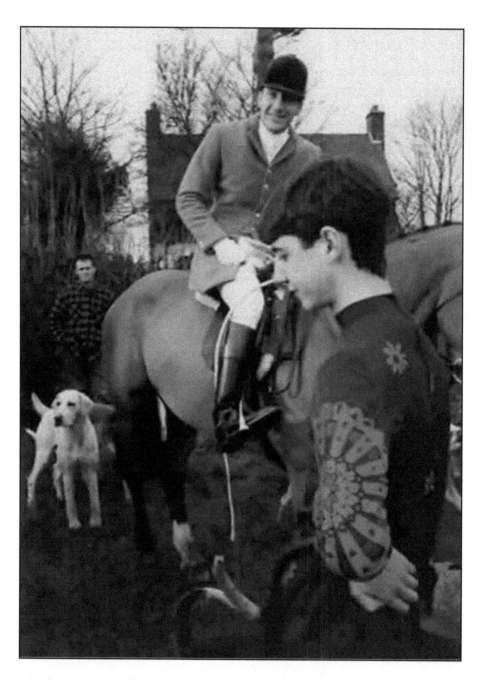

RAGE FOR THE MACHINE - *Here is pre-hospital **Roderick Wilson** (far left in chequered shirt) glaring with intent behind the Master of Foxhounds Vale of Aylesbury Foxhunt. The chap in the purple garb is a sab. We didn't usually dress like this. The photo was taken on the day when we all dressed up in drag to emphasize Drag hunting as an alternative to fox hunting. It clearly worked because since the ban on hunting with dogs in the UK, drag hunting is the only permissible type of hunting allowed. source Authors personal collection.*

'FUCK' THE POLICE! – IN BED WITH THE ENEMY

UK STATE INFILTRATION OF THE MOVEMENT. *there's never a policeman around when you need one. Or is there?*

They made the Stasi look like mere Peeping Toms. They directly helped carry out some of the biggest animal rights actions ever seen, including, allegedly, arson. Some went mad. Some went native. One of them even co-wrote the infamous 'What's wrong with McDonalds' leaflets that triggered the longest civil trial in UK history, the McLibel trial.

Say Hello to the Special Demonstration Squad (SDS). AKA 'The Hairies'. AKA That New Person in the group offering everyone a lift in their van. Say another 'HI' to its grotesque conjoined twin, the National Public Order Intelligence Unit (NPOIU). Every bit as ideologically driven as the KGB or Stasi were in their day, this evil pair were loosed upon a thoroughly unsuspecting civil society in 1969.

COUNTER-EVOLUTIONARIES - When Mark Kennedy/AKA 'Mark Stone' admitted to being a spy cop in 2010, it was a shock. Everyone knew there was spying and infiltration of 'the movement' but no-one realised just how deep it went.

Kennedy was a well-known figure in 'radical environmentalist' groups for ten years, both in the UK and abroad, including Ireland.

It's known he was involved in planning the 2004 anti-EU protests in Dublin, with its attendant 'push' bloc. It's likely he had a sneaky look at the thriving anarchist/eco-scene active in Ireland at the time, possibly visiting the anti-Shell Oil protest camp in Rossport. Because the current Public Inquiry into Police spies has limited its scope of interest to England and Wales only, we may never know the details. There were also many spies sent in by Corporations and of course Informers but these are outside the scope of this Inquiry.

We do know what Kennedy and 138 others were getting up to in England and Wales and we can extrapolate from there.

Between 1968 and 2008 when the SDS was disbanded, 1000 political/social protest groups were infiltrated by undercover police, only 3 of which were far-right groups. Most of the remaining 997 were left leaning/left wing groups of various hues. The rest were single issue social justice type campaigns.

Police explained they were reluctant to spy on the far right "because they are too violent"! One would have though this the perfect reason *to* spy on them.

Many of these cops went *deep* undercover, for years at a time, forming intimate relationships and some (4) even having children with their 'targets'. They stole the names of dead children to use as their undercover identities.

To gain credibility, many cops committed crimes/direct actions, or aided and abetted criminality/direct action, sometimes on a vast scale. In fact, some of the biggest and most successful animal rights actions ever carried out in the UK were enabled, or directly committed, by the police.

In 1993, spycop 'Matt Rayner' drove 7 animal rights activists to the Grand National horse race at Aintree in 'his' van, essentially an unmarked police vehicle. Those 7 activists joined 8 others and gained access to the racecourse seconds before the race was due to begin. They formed a human blockade across it. They caused absolute chaos and were thrown out. They immediately broke back in and did it again. More Chaos, including false starts. This disruption prevented the race from starting at all and cost the horse betting industry $75 MILLION in returned bets, the biggest amount of financial damage from a single piece of direct action ever. No charges were brought against the activists. They weren't even asked to chip in for petrol costs by 'Rayner'! Thanks, cops!

above – *the man we have to thank for the unveiling of the spycops scandal – Mark Kennedy AKA Mark 'Stone' posing as an eco-anarchist. His unmasking in 2010 set the ball rolling as journalists and activists uncovered more and more police spies in the movement, dating back to the 1960's. Over a 7-year period, Kennedy (as Stone) visited 22 other countries to help plan and take part in direct action, including (allegedly) arson in Germany. He was at the violent Dublin Mayday demo in 2004, where he (allegedly) encouraged other activists to attack Police. The Irish Government knew of and approved his presence, as did the States of the other countries he travelled to. With his voice-recording Casio watch and his Handler always nearby, Kennedy weaselled his way into the Earth First movement in Nottingham by having a van and always being ready to drive people to and from actions, home addresses and squatted social centres. In 2006, Kennedy was at a demonstration outside Drax power station when he saw a 'fellow' female activist being attacked by five policemen. When Kennedy stepped in to help her, he too was beaten mercilessly, suffering broken bones and a prolapsed disc.stock image.*

"I experienced a lot of unjust policing. At times, I was appalled at being a police officer." Said Kennedy about his time undercover.

Kennedy was so appalled by his betrayal, so upset at witnessing 'good friends' being brutalised by police, that he now works for nefarious Multi-National Corporations advising them on how to deal with protest groups. There's Redemption in action for you.

Kennedys links with Ireland are many - his Irish (ex) wife still resides in her native Kanturk and Kennedy, as Mark Stone, visited the Shell-to-Sea protest camp as well as numerous Dublin-based actions including the Mayday riot in 2004 in Dublin where he "was to the fore wearing a balaclava and violently attacking police" according to one activist as reported in the Irish Examiner in 2011.

"I hate myself so much , I betrayed so many people. I owe it to a lot of good people to do something right for a change...I'm really sorry". UK spycop Mark Kennedy in a taped phone call to an activist he spied upon, 2010. We hate you too, Mark.

Some of the biggest fires seen in Britain since World War Two were started by the Animal Liberation Front. And at least one (allegedly) was started by an undercover cop known to his 'friends' as Bob Robinson, who infiltrated the ALF during the 1980's at the peak of their highly successful war on the fur trade.

In 1987, Robinson, real name Bob Lambert, was part of a three-man ALF cell who were targeting department stores selling fur. Their tactic was to use small homemade incendiary devices that would be placed behind flammable furniture in the selected shop. Timed to ignite when the store was closed, the small fire produced by the incendiary device would trigger the buildings sprinkler system. The resultant flood would put out the fire but ruin the shops stock.

One night in July, three London Debenhams stores were targeted. Lambert (allegedly) planted his incendiary device in a Debenhams in Harrow. The incendiary ignited a fire at around midnight, activating the buildings sprinkler system. This put the fire out but caused $340,000 in water damaged goods.

One of the other Debenhams targeted that night was not so lucky – the Luton Debenhams sprinkler system wasn't working, and the building burned to the ground. Debenhams stopped selling fur following these actions.

Lambert got promotion. The other two – Geoff Shepherd and Andrew Clarke - got 7 years between them.

Lambert wrote the book on underhand undercover policing. Literally. After 4 years pretending to be a fire-bombing vegan anarchist, fathering a child in the process, Lambert retired from active duty and authored the Special Demonstration Squads Tradecraft Manuel. This manual described a 'by any means necessary' approach and was used as a template for the likes of Mark Kennedy and many others. Twenty-four years later, in 2014, Lamberts 'undercover' son and partner both successfully sued the Metropolitan Police for psychological damages caused by Lamberts' deceptions. The woman, 'Jacqui' received $425,000, the son a similar amount.

Lambert even co-wrote the infamous 'What's wrong with McDonalds?' leaflet, distributed in their millions for years by grassroots activists like me outside McDonalds restaurants the world over. The leaflet McDonalds sued two London Greenpeace activists over in one of the longest Civil Trials and biggest own goals in Corporate history. Co-written by a secret *cop*.

Lambert retired from the Metropolitan Police in 2007 and in 2008 was made a Member of the British Empire. He took up a few cushy, lucrative positions in Universities where he reinvented himself as an academic. This creep was laughing all the way to the bank until his exposure in 2011. Ex-London Greenpeace members publicly confronted him as he was delivering a lecture in London. Lambert was absolutely stunned by the sudden appearance of his old 'marks' and when they began firing questions at him, he got up and ran out of the hall. On the streets he was apprehended again by the activists he once spied upon. Trying his best to ignore their questions he squeezed into a cab and sped off.

His life would never be the same again. As more and more shocking facts came to light, Lambert's career as a polished intellectual was over. Over the next few years, he was forced to resign from his University posts and has essentially disappeared from academia and public life.

But you didn't need to be an ALF arsonist to attract Police attention. And it wasn't only male cops doing the spying.

There are 3 known female undercover cops and one of them occasionally spied on our group of Hunt Saboteurs.

above - **LOOK OUT BEHIND YOU!** - *Friend and fellow saboteur Rod looks back at undercover cop 'Christine Green' as she helps us sabotage a Vale of Aylesbury hunt circa 1997. In their efforts to gain credibility, Police spies regularly assisted animal rights activists in their endeavours, much more than they'd care to admit. 'Christine' had a reputation for being a feisty, aggressive saboteur, unafraid to get stuck in if required. 'John Dines', another spycop who infiltrated the London hunt sab movement, was also considered to be handy to have around in a tight spot - "He could handle himself when we had stand-offs and punch-ups with Hunt supporters in Surrey and Sussex and he was actually good to have around" said one Sab of his experiences saving foxes with him. (HOWL#123, p. 32) source HSA archive.*

'Christine Green' (real name unknown) infiltrated the West London Hunt Saboteurs throughout the mid-to-late 1990's, a group we- the Chiltern Hunt Sabs- often teamed up and sabbed with.

'Christine' was known to be aggressive and 'shouty' when out sabbing, and an excellent (police trained) driver who often drove the sab van. She was arrested once for aggravated trespass at a hunt, but the charges were later dropped.

Christine also campaigned with various animal rights campaigns across London, both legal and otherwise.

In 1999 she took part in the largest ALF raid in UK history – helping release 6000 minks from a fur farm in the New Forest. She also began going out with a prominent West London hunt sab by the name of Tom Frampton. Tom was an enthusiastic campaigner and had served time in prison for head-butting a fox hunter in 1994.

In 2000, after 5 years undercover and deployment over, she simply disappeared. Her uncle had died, she said, and left her some money and she was "off to Australia for six months."

While away, Christine quietly quit her job with the Police. She also got in touch with Frampton and the two hooked up again when she returned to the UK. They moved to Cornwall where she got a job at a Rape Crisis Centre and Tom continued animal rights work.

'Christine' had gone native. This must have mightily pissed off the Met. There was surely many a sleepless night spent by her former colleagues, worried at what police secrets she might be divulging to her activist lover.

Her previous life as a police spy hadn't yet been made public but when the first allegations against Mark Kennedy emerged in 2010, She and Tom discreetly moved to rural Ayrshire in Scotland, exact whereabouts unknown. The couple, ex-cop and her erstwhile 'target', have remained together and under the radar ever since.

"Some of the best friends anyone could ever want, people who without hesitation put their liberty and sometimes their life on the line for me".

'Christine Green', undercover cop, on those she spied upon.

The Guardian newspaper finally exposed 'Christine' years later. As more and more spies were exposed from 2010 on, patterns emerged. Her 'pattern' was compared to exposed spies like Mark Kennedy by those who suspected her as a cop back in the 1990's and was found to be remarkably similar - Appears suddenly with a vague back story (or 'legend'),'lives' in a sparsely furnished apartment (no-one actually lives there), owns a van (unusual amongst activists those days), is always eager to drive people around (to find out where you live),is very good at driving (police training), has no obvious employment but always has cash, is friendly and inquisitive, has arranged themselves into group admin roles (gaining access to internal documents) and disappears suddenly without trace after 4-5 years…. It's as though they all read the same rule book. The one written by Bob Lambert.

Further investigation by the Guardian and others confirmed suspicions and it all went public in 2017.

Revenge being a dish best served cold, her previous employers at the Metropolitan Police then made a public statement, confirming her role as an undercover police agent and implicating her in the 1999 ALF mink farm raid.

'Christine' quickly retaliated with a public statement of her own, lambasting the Police and apologising "to those activists I was closest to and who befriended me, opening their lives and their homes to me…. some of the best friends anyone could ever want, people who without hesitation put their liberty and sometimes their life on the line for me".

Given the benign goals and tactics of the hunt sabotage movement, the State seemed highly aroused and concerned by it all.

The most a group of Saboteurs were going to do was follow a Hunt and mimic their voice and horn calls and defend themselves in the process. Essentially, do the same as the hunt. This may, or may not, result in a fox escaping the jaws of hounds. That's it. Hardly storming the Bastille.

Yet the Police spent millions endlessly spying on and harassing the movement. New laws were drafted to outlaw activism, existing laws were regularly broken by the Police who then paid out hundreds of thousands in successful compensation claims by hunt Sabs. Seemingly unlimited resources were poured into 'defending' the Elite's 'right' to Hunt and they were never asked for a penny in contribution, despite being amongst the wealthiest people in the country.

Mounted police, Riot Police, Police in helicopters, spycops, extra police powers, private security firms, you name it they got it. And it still didn't work.

Groups like the Brixton Hunt Saboteurs had a steady succession of police spies entering and leaving their ranks throughout the 1990's, and possibly earlier. 'Christine' tried to gain the trust of the Brixton group at the very start of her deployment in 1995 but was suspected even then and given the cold shoulder. She was meant to take over from spycop 'Andy Davey' who was himself under suspicion.

'TO PROTEST AND PERV' - 'Andy Davey', AKA Andy Coles, had been spying on the Brixton Sabs for four years in the early 1990's and had struck up a relationship with a considerably younger female activist. However, his generally unsavoury behaviour alienated him from those he was trying to ingratiate himself with. Coles was in his mid-thirties, significantly older than most of his 'targets', some of whom were still in their teens, including his 'girlfriend'. He was described as sleezy and pervy, making unwanted advances and creeping people out. He wasn't coming up with golden nuggets of information because no one trusted or liked him. This made its way back to his bosses at the Met and he was withdrawn early from active service. This lacklustre (at best) performance did not stop him from being promoted to Head of Training for future spycops.

Coles left the Police in 2012 as the Spycops scandal was breaking but found a natural home in the Conservative Party, becoming a Tory Councillor at Peterborough Council for several years. He also worked as the Deputy Police and Crime Commissioner for Cambridge and Peterborough. Not bad for someone whose resume consists mainly of being an underperforming spy.

"A weirdo outsider...hearts would sink at the sight of him, but we also felt sorry for him" Shirley, Brixton hunt sab, describing top cop sleuth Andy "Davey".

And he might have got away with it, enjoying his fat police pension, plus his salaries as Deputy Crime Commissioner and Councillor.

He might have got away with it if his brother hadn't written that damn book. But he did write it. And people read it. And they put two and two together and in 2017 Andy Coles career came crashing down around him.

Cole's brother, Richard, was none other than one half of pop duo the Communards, a successful synth-pop band from the 1980's. Champions of Gay rights and all-round disco-loving lefties, the Communards had a large gay following during their heyday. In 2017, Richard Coles (now an Anglican Vicar) published his autobiography 'Fathomless Riches' where he innocently describes his brother thus: *"My older brother Andy brought his own drama with him. He looked like he had just walked out of the woods, his hair all long and shaggy, with a scraggly beard, his ears rattling with piercings. But his disarray was not like mine – an outward sign of internal distress – but suffered in the line of duty. He had joined Special Branch and was undercover, living a double life, infiltrated into some sinister organisation while his wife and baby daughter made do with unpredictable visits."*

Oops! Richard Coles, the gay Vicar, had just outed his brother without even knowing it. God indeed works in mysterious ways.

The book sold well, and it wasn't long till some synth-pop loving animal rights activist stumbled across the incriminating paragraph. The Guardian and the Undercover

Research Group were both tipped off and after more investigations went public with the news.

Within two hours of the news going public, Coles had resigned his position as Deputy Police and Crime Commissioner. He clung on to his position as a City Councillor until 2022's elections when he was dropped as a candidate by his Party. Even the Tories, when given the choice, seem to prefer their Candidates with a less publicly pervy and dysfunctional past.

above left - **Andy Coles** incognito as a Brixton hunt saboteur (with hat, sleeveless jacket, third from left) attending a hunt with unwitting girlfriend 'Jessica' and the Brixton Mob. Source HSA archive.

- right – Andy's brothers' book ("Fathomless Riches") about his life in the Communards. The book mentions Andy in passing and this was read by some of the people Andy spied on. He had long been suspected by many and now there was proof. Stock image.

Here's the offending article- "My older brother Andy brought his own drama with him. He looked like he had just walked out of the woods, his hair long and shaggy, with a straggly beard, his ears rattling with piercings: but his disarray was not like mine, an outward sign of mental distress, but suffered in the line of duty. He had joined Special Branch and was undercover, living a double life, infiltrated into some sinister organisation while his wife and baby daughter made do with unpredictable visits."

There were many more spies in the animal rights/environmental movement throughout the 1980's and beyond, each with their own bizarre and sinister goings-on. The three examples above illustrate sharply the mentality and tactics of these people. It also illustrates just what how threatened the Establishment is by the animal rights /environmental movement.

How much of this went on in Ireland is as yet unknown. Four spycops are known to have spent time here during their deployments - Mark Kennedy, Jim Boyling, Mark Jenner and John Dines.

We also know that policemen who worked as spies for the SDS went on to teach their skills to police forces around the world – Spycop John Dines, for instance, now works at the Australian Graduate School of Security training police spies there and in India on how to infiltrate left wing groups.

Much more will come out as the Public Inquiry progresses, but it will be confined to England and Wales only. Their refusal to include Scotland or Ireland in their scope speaks volumes. Despite its shortcomings, at least the Public Inquiry offers us insight into what they were doing elsewhere.

There's so much more to be written about the Spycops scandal and I encourage anyone to check out the ongoing Inquiry online at Police Spies Out of Our Lives and elsewhere.

However, it's worth noting just how corrupt and ideologically driven the whole undercover police operation was from the start – every bit as political as their KGB counterparts in the Soviet Union of old.

Ostensibly, the Police exist to investigate crime and prosecute criminals.

By contrast, the SDS's mission was to build up a database of left wing and progressive movements so these movements could be stifled and strangled by any nefarious means necessary. It mattered not if these groups were typically open and entirely peaceful with usually admirable goals and legal methods.

 Very few actual arrests were made and the it's possible the SDS participated in more crimes than they prevented. The SDS were profoundly anti-democratic in their behaviour and reflected the actions of a Police State, not a Police Service.

Not one Spycop has faced intimidation or violence from those whose lives were so brutally intruded upon and damaged. The only violence they experienced was when they were attacked by their own side. At environmental protests and anti-fascist rallies, at the Poll Rax riots and animal rights actions, many a spycop has told the Enquiry of how they were viciously beaten by baton-wielding cops who were unaware they were attacking colleagues. It's almost like they were *spying on the wrong side*....

This is how Spycop John Dines described his experience getting beaten and arrested by uniformed co-workers when he was undercover as a Class War anarchist at the infamous Poll Tax riot in London 1990 – he was asked to write up his experiences for a publication called 'Poll Tax Riot – ten hours that shook the world'. Here he is describing the scene in central London upon his release from the police cells, some hours after the riot was over:

154

"The shattered windows of the South African Embassy further lifted my spirits, and I couldn't resist an ear-to-ear grin as a mob of miserable cops walked towards me, peering out from under the brims of their helmets, hunched shoulders, literally 'plodding' along. Though I had missed it, I knew the bastards (the police) *had taken a real good hiding."*

I wonder if any of his battered colleagues read his description of them that day – must have made for awkward conversation round the police station canteen table later on.

above – *undercover cop 'John Dines' (real surname Barker) at a hunt with 'fellow' activists. Location unknown, circa 1990. Source HSA archive.*
This guy had a 'relationship' with McLibel defendant Helen Steel throughout the period of the McLibel Trial. He now lives in Australia where he teaches Indian police how to infiltrate left wing movements in India. A real piece of shit. Handy in a punch-up though and likes a good riot.

AUSTIN POWERS MEETS GOLLUM - One can only wonder at the psychological make-up of the average Special Demonstration Squad Officer. Deception, gaslighting and betrayal were just another day at the office for these guys.

One female spycop was sent to infiltrate and undermine a Women's Rights group who were campaigning for equal pay with men. All the while she was being paid less than her male colleagues. Is this what she joined the Police for?

They were, in effect, above the law and broke it regularly with impunity. Actions that got activists sent to prison for years brought these guys promotion. It was no law for them and draconian laws for everyone else.

The Inquiry expects to publish its findings in 2027.

The 'work' of the SDS is now done by the secretive National Domestic Extremism Unit. Little is known about them. Despite changes in the law and policy, and the massive loss of public trust, it's seems unlikely to this author at least that the Police have changed their behaviour, either institutionally or individually.

Their heel-dragging at every pivotal point leading up to and during the Inquiry tells us all we need to know about their 'commitment' to change. The Inquiry -established in 2015 –didn't get properly started until 2021 because of Police delay tactics. They wasted 3 years alone trying to secure anonymity for their officers. Like fellow-travellers the Catholic Church, the Bottom line is Perception Management. So is the Top Line.

FORWARDS! TOWARD A BENEVORIAN FUTURE!

The end of their world is nigh! the Fifth Wave (2015- 2022-ish) and the emerging Sixth Wave.

There were many attempts to describe people who deliberately avoid animal 'products' before the term "Vegan" was settled on in 1944 by Donald Watson and the newly formed Vegan Society of Great Britain. Alternatives proposed include DAIRYBAN, BENEVORE, PYTHAGAORAN, GRAHAMITE (After Rev. Sylvester Graham, a US vegan from the 19th century), VITAN, BEAUMANGEUR, SANIVORE, NEO-VEGETARIAN and my personal favourite - as suggested by the Irish Press in 1949- SUPER-VEGETARIAN.

above - *early pioneer of the Pythagorist Benevorean diet,* **Mr Donald Watson**, *co-inventor of the term 'vegan' and a passionate Dairybanner. Donald also helped establish the Vegan Society when the Vegetarian Society, then almost a century old, refused to allow a 'non-ovo/lacto vegetarian' (i.e., vegan) wing of the Society. Stock image.*

So, in 1944, one of the most violent years in human history, the UK Vegan Society was established - the first of its kind and the spearhead of a quiet (then shouty) social revolution. The original Peace movement. The Vegetarian Society's refusal to recognise veganism as a strand within the movement was a blessing in disguise as it forced vegans to carve out their own niche and establish an independent position, separate from vegetarianism, as it should be.

When asked what advice he had for young vegans, Watson replied **"I would like them to take a broad view of what veganism stands for. I would like them to realise they're onto something really big."**

A man truly ahead of both the curve and his time.

above – *"Yes! It's porridge for dinner again! Pass the salt!"* artists impression of a typical Sanivorian family circa mid-20th century. Followers of the Grahamite diet, circa 1948. Note the crisp sangwitches in the centre, a classic Beaumangeurian staple of the period. Stock image.

SLOWLY AT FIRST, THEN ALL OF A SUDDEN –

2015. This was the year when interest in, and embracement of, veganism began to grow dramatically. This was the beginning of the Fifth Wave of the fight against violence against animals in Ireland. Young people, particularly females, started showing a strong interest in the health and environmental benefits of "plant-based eating" and it's been on a roll ever since. This unprecedented uptick happened more or less simultaneously in many countries across the globe, Ireland included.

In fact, over the last five years, Ireland has come in the top ten of numerous 'most vegan-friendly countries' lists, with Dublin recently topping a global list of best cities for vegans. (2019 Hayes and Jarvis).

"The likelihood seems to be that Westerners will be eating a diet which is much less meaty in the future...The farmers, meanwhile, will eat their hearts out". Prophetic words from journalist Lucile Redmond, Irish Times, April 15, 1978.

In 2018, Ireland's State Food Board, Bord Bia, commissioned a major report into the changing eating habits and priorities of the population- the Dietary Lifestyles Report. Bord Bia exist to promote Irish goods, particularly meat and dairy, and they hadn't failed to notice a continuing shift away from their prized produce. Keen to get to the bottom of this, they repeated the study in 2021 and the results are fascinating, particularly when compared to each other. This Report was part of a wider study that took in 8 other western European countries and China and the figures below match closely across the board.

The 2018 study found that 4.1% (150,000) of the Irish population *associated* with the vegan diet, 8% with vegetarian and another 10.6 % with Flexitarian. These numbers are undoubtedly an exponential increase from any time before and they increased dramatically in the 3 years since that report was published.

Bord Bia's *latest* Dietary Report - from March 2021 - notes the percentage of people *associating* with the Vegan diet in Ireland increased over threefold to a whopping 14% by 2020. The amount associating with Vegetarianism and Flexitarianism both almost doubled to 14% and 19% respectively. That's essentially half of Irelands population trending away from animal products, either completely or partially, and that number will only have since increased.

Under the reports separate heading *"Adherence* to this diet in terms of food consumption/behaviour", the numbers are significantly lower, but still significant. Between the 2018 report and 2021 report, vegan food consumption more than quadrupled from 0.4% to 2% of the Nation's total food consumption, for Vegetarians it went from 6% to 8% and for Flexitarians it rose from 10% to 16%.

In short, over one quarter (26%) of Irish people in 2020 had deliberately eliminated or significantly reduced their consumption of animal flesh and fluids, and another quarter are on their way.

As stated, because it's worth repeating, these are highly significant numbers in themselves, and huge increases from the recent past, and will inevitably be higher again by now, 2023.

Percentages of a population required to effect significant change in a modern democratic society vary, but a common ball-park figure is between 25-30%. These are also the numbers that get Political parties elected to office.

Is Irish society and State at, or vey near, this tipping point? The statistics say yes.

Veganism- in Ireland and elsewhere - has gone from being an almost invisible – and much mocked - niche concern to becoming a rival to the mainstream in the space of an average human life.

Current trends imply veganism *will be* the mainstream within a decade, at least in the 'post-industrial' parts of the world. No one is more surprised about all this than the pre-existing Vegan community.

This Fifth Wave is cause for celebration and stands in stark contrast to how things were. It wasn't long ago when almost everyone assumed eating animal flesh and drinking bovine secretions was vital for survival. Practically everyone I knew warned me off giving up meat when I was 13. My Parents, my sisters, our family GP, my friends, their siblings and their Parents, schoolteachers, even our local parish Priest. They all had their say and it was all negative. People were practically queuing up to tell me I'd be dead in six months if I didn't eat meat. And that was just going *vegetarian*. I don't recall meeting anyone with anything good to say about the issue until I met fellow -vegetarians and vegans some years after making the switch.

We now know, of course, that a plant-based diet is extremely good for the human body. The vegan diet is the only diet proven to *reverse* heart disease, it can dramatically increase Life span and Health span. Risk from a range of common ailments, cancers and diseases is greatly reduced, typically by 25-30%. Recovery from injury is quicker. The body feels lighter. You stop seeing animals as future shit-coffins and more as fellow-travellers.

The "Four N's" of justification for animal agriculture have been assailed and defeated, at least to those who look at this objectively. Jared Piazza, a Senior Lecturer at Lancaster University, identified four psychological props commonly used in defence of meat and milk consumption: 'Meat and Milk Are **Nice, Natural, Necessary** and (crucially) **Normal**.

These are the nebulous buzz words used by the Animal Agriculture to legitimise their behaviour.

Each buzz word comes with its own half-truths and myths firmly baked in.

All have been exposed and challenged like never before. Science and commerce, activism and social media – have all have been utilised by the vegan movement to dismantle those old tropes.

Top athletes in a range of sports praise the benefits it bestows. Actors and Philosophers, Musicians and Politicians, (ex) Royalty and Anarchists, endorse veganism for all sorts of valid reasons.

Vegan protein alternatives are now *accessible, affordable,* and *attractive* like never before. The sense of the *Normality* of veganism, one of the biggest obstacles to its uptake and a key reason why people stop being vegan, is finally shifting. Although the formalised concept has been in existence since 1944, the widespread promotion of it is much newer, really only coming to the fore in the 1990's. Before then, it was rare to find a vegan even within a lot of animal rights groups. The issue was often avoided by campaigners as it was perceived to be too much of an ask and would only put people off. Now it's a core principle of the movement and has made huge inroads into mainstream culture. The speed of this spread has taken everybody, particularly the vegans, by surprise. And it can't happen fast enough.

In our relentlessly idiotic attempt to produce food in the most cruel and inefficient means available to us, we have turned our world into a cesspit. A societal shift to a plant-based diet is an essential component of any strategy to preserve viable human society on our planet, just as vital as (and a vital part of) the shift to carbon-neutral energy and the reintroduction of biodiversity.

It's also the one change that most individuals can make instantly and easily. The much-quoted statistic that animal agriculture is responsible for about 18% of the worlds carbon emissions is a gross understatement that ignores so many aspects of this catastrophic industry. Not included in this figure is the carbon that was released when the farmland was cleared so cattle could be grazed on it, nor how much carbon would be absorbed by the same farmland if it was still forested. Now apply the same metric to all the farmlands being used to grow crops that are then fed to the livestock. Also ignored is the vast industrial system and transport requirements of the industry. When all of this is factored in, as it should be, the figure is much higher, between 30-50% (1) of global carbon emissions, depending on the study and geographical area. And that's just the carbon. Factor in nitrates and methane and animal agriculture stands out as a leading, if not *the* leading, cause of environmental collapse.

In the country I'm writing this book from, New Zealand, animal ag produces a whopping 44% of the nation's greenhouse gases, while employing a mere 3% of the workforce. This Government estimate, high as it is, does not factor in the fact that Kiwi dairy farmers feed their herd palm oil kernels as standard, a product imported thousands of miles from the decimated rainforests of Indonesia. Nor does it account for the fact that 80% of the milk produced is then dried out, using coal-fired power stations, then shipped to China, so the real figure must be considerably higher.

A study by Climate Healers estimated animal agriculture is responsible for 87% of the world's greenhouse gas emissions (2). Like a coprophilic King Midas of myth, whose mere touch turned things to gold, everything animal agriculture touches turns to shit.

PRESICION FERMENTATION – Two seemingly innocuous words that, when combined in this order, are potent in the extreme. Keeping dairy farmers awake at night and getting vegan entrepreneurs out of bed in the morning. A soon-to-be cheaper and infinitely more efficient way of obtaining milk proteins. More than efficient enough to send the dairy industry packing. Most milk produced in the EU is dried to a powder and sold to food manufacturers to be used as whey in confectionary. *Moo*vers (ha ha) in this new industry reckon they'll have eclipsed the traditional dairy sector within this decade.

Precision Fermentation is set to out -perform dairy milk production at every level – cheaper, much quicker, sustainable, cruelty-free and can be produced almost anywhere.

Precision Fermentation works in a similar way to brewing beer or baking bread – a way of multiplying microbes to produce, in this case, milk protein identical to those found in cow's milk.

No more wasting ***eleven thousand*** litres of clean water to produce ***one*** litre of milk. No more reducing local biodiversity to just ***one*** species of grass feeding just ***one*** species of animal. An end to that ultimate cruelty of stealing babies from their mothers. No more poisoned fields, dead rivers and dying biosphere.

Am I Lactose intolerant? Absolutely, and not just to lactose. The entire dairy industry makes my blood boil and my skin crawl.

Also, I'm not a baby cow.

The current capitalist-dominant ideology that drives our financial and social systems is doomed to follow the Soviet Union model and collapse under the weight of its own contradictions. It already collapsed in 2007 due to financial reasons of course but got bailed out by the taxpayer. Now it's collapsing because of environmental reasons, and that cannot be bailed out. The fallacies of Individuality, Externality and Infinite Growth have all but exhausted our planets carrying capacity. We are now the proverbial frog in the pot of heating water, gradually being boiled alive yet remaining static, except we don't have ignorance as an excuse.

Unlike the laws of commerce, The Laws of Nature are non-negotiable - Everything is connected; matter cannot be destroyed, only rearranged; all growth is limited.

We now face oblivion because reality was ignored in favour of ideology and short-term convenience.

Individuality, the delusion of the Self-made person, is a spell.

Everything and everyone, to a greater or lesser extent, is connected to everything and everyone else.

Externality, the self-serving notion that undesirable end results of production and consumption– namely pollution - can be dumped somewhere far away and safely ignored. Out of sight out of mind.

Infinite Growth on a finite Planet? The absurdity of this proposition is immediately obvious to all but the most ideologically blinkered of economists. Economists, and wankers.

One of the biggest obstacles we face is the fact that so many people just can't imagine how bad things are likely to get unless we quickly change and adapt our behaviour as a species. The tragedies and holocausts already set in motion are barrelling downhill toward us and yet, despite the mounting evidence and all the alarm bells going off at once, most people completely underestimate what's soon to hit us with the force of a speeding train.

When the gravity and consequences of a phenomena are too terrible to accept, or even imagine, we hide behind platitudes and elusions, rejecting an awful reality for a more desired outcome. We, as a society, have engaged in this level of denial for years and have finally run out of road. The message is now clear – Adapt or Die.

This quickly growing realisation is the driving factor behind the emerging Sixth Wave of animal rights in Ireland and elsewhere. This Wave will be characterised by a dramatic uptick in State and Corporate intervention in animal agriculture and consumption as they incentivise a shift away from animal exploitation and toward sustainable, plant-based produce.

The direct-action wing of the animal movement will continue to openly and defiantly challenge the industry at every level, including at the consumer end with activists occupying and blockading restaurants and markets. 'Cultured' meat and fermented milk produce will become widely available, pushing animal 'produce' to the edges of society, consumed only by a die-hard few. The vital rewilding of ex-fharmland will become commonplace as we seek to reintroduce vital biodiversity and increase carbon capture. We might even see some of the most egregious offenders in our

War against Nature in the Dock facing charges and prison time, an Eco-Nuremburg Trials. This shift will be largely led by today's youth as they mature and, essentially, 'become' the System. In time, this Sixth Wave in the evolution of our relations with other animals will be considered as significant to our Species as the Industrial and Agricultural Revolutions were.

"How far are you prepared to go?" was a question often put to animal rights activists following the latest 'outrage' or other. What if we put that question to those who continue to devour animal flesh and bovine secretions?

"To the end(s) of the Earth" can be their only honest response because that's where they're taking us. The last-and really only – defence of their behaviour is that "I've been doing this for ages, and it tastes nice". That's it. Everything else can get 'externalised.' And if you don't agree with them, you're somehow both a communist *and* a fascist. I used to think such behaviour showed indifference at best, callousness at worst.

Now it seems it's also suicidally, genocidally stupid. People are making an informed choice to eat their -and Your- future alive because of unwillingness to adapt their diet. Surely this is self-murdering nihilism on a scale not seen before. And they have the star-studded fucking audacity to call *us* extreme.

   (1)   www.awellfedworld.org/wp-content/uploads/Livestock-Climate-Change-Anhang-Goodland.pdf

   (2) www.climatehealers.org/the-science/animal-agriculture-position-paper/

"People don't like to dwell on the animal origins of their meal, and modern meat production is strategically designed to help consumers forget." J. Piazza, The Psychologist, volume-34, January 2021. We're here to remind them.

Those who are reminded of history are more likely to repeat it.

Action is the Antidote to Despair.

The End

Of their World

Is Nigh

FURTHER RECOMMENDED READING – sources and resources

The following is a list of books that further explore the dynamic history of strident animal activism on the islands of Britain and Ireland.

Animals in Irish Society- *Interspecies oppression and vegan liberation in Britains first colony.*

Corey Lee Wrenn, 2021, Suny Press. The only other book exploring Irelands historical relationships with non-human animals from a vegan perspective.

From Dusk 'til Dawn: *An Insider's View of the Growth of the Animal Liberation Movement.*

Keith Mann, 2007, Puppy Pincher Press. Keith was sentenced to 14 years imprisonment for ALF actions in 1991 and spent a lot of that time writing this 700-page tome.

Sabotage – *the story of the Hunt Saboteurs Association.*

Dazza Scott, 2021. Available from the HSA website. The official history of the mighty HSA. Large size book with excellent photographs.

Outfoxed – *a factual account of 'sporting' activities in the countryside.*

Mike Huskisson, 1983. Available from the HSA website.

Outfoxed Again – *winning for animals 1984-2005.*

Mike Huskisson, 2017. Available from the HSA website. Mikes books detail his many years in the UK undercover posing as a blood-sports enthusiast and as an animal activist who spent time in prison for his actions.

The Animals Freedom Fighter – *a biography of Ronnie Lee, founder of the Animal Liberation Front.*

Jon Hochschartner, 2017.

Undercover – *the true story of Britain's secret police.*

Rob Evans and Paul Louis, 2014. Two top Guardian journalists investigate and expose the reality and impact of the UK's very own Stasi on the environmental movement.

Websites

https://www.thehumanitytrigger.com/

http://thetalonconspiracy.com/

https://www.huntsabs.org.uk/

https://naracampaigns.org/

https://www.facebook.com/allianceforanimalrights/

https://thehappypear.ie/

https://irishvegan.ie/

https://www.facebook.com/theveganinformationproject

https://goveganworld.com/

https://www.facebook.com/AnimalRebellionIreland/

https://www.irishnewsarchive.com/

ABOUT THE AUTHOR

Mark Humanity is a long-time vegan activist. He currently lives on the edge of a rainforest in New Zealand and is on the Board of the Vegan Society of Aotearoa, New Zealand.

The Author and daughter about to join an animal rights march, Auckland 2019.